THE COMEDYPHILES

Stephen Hoover & L.A. Laird

THE CONJURER

Dedicated to my daughter, Eva, who always makes me smile.

- *STH*

The Comedyphiles

Book design and cover layout by: Cat Stewart

Illustrations & cover art by: Jonathan Brown

ISBN:978-0-9897465-4-0

TABLE OF CONTENTS

FOREWARD: AN INTRODUCTION

If the following collection of material at times seems sophomoric, it's because it is. Sophomore in college, to be precise. This is when I began the process of writing sketches in notebooks during breaks and occasionally in classes for the amusement of my friends. One such friend, L.A. Laird, became a co-writer and worked on all of the material collected here. The shorts and screenplay included were from this early period of the mid-90s.

One wit once quipped that writing was like sex. First you do it for yourself, then a few friends, and after awhile you're doing it for money. We sadly never got to the money part. Law books replaced joke books as I took what seemed the more reasonable path of becoming an attorney.

Our career did have a few highlights: Material performed on CBS by a comedian who paid us per joke. The comedian later performed several jokes on a cable network and asked why he hadn't paid us for the material responded he was "trying the jokes out." Several cartoon gags appeared in national magazines.

We also were signed by an agent who was well known in the industry as a nobody. One contact with a production company by myself about sending over material in which I mentioned his name led to the response, "We know him. He's a nobody." After a few months of getting us nowhere but not without charging us for expenses, such as copies, mail, his dry cleaning.

After a break pursuing my legal career, we returned to writing and material such as the sitcom pilot and a few other sketches were from this period around 2005. This was further fueled by the optioning of a screenplay and several of my wins in national contests.

I read recently that the average writer gets paid 10 cents per hour. That's a healthy estimation of my pay thus far. But writers are an odd lot. A mix of courage and fear, ego and self doubt. We pursue our passion because that's part of our nature.

With good things on the way for me next year and feature film or films heading to production, this collection is a look back with a smile. This is also intended to be a companion piece to my other book THE JOKE'S ON YOU: HOW TO WRITE COMEDY.

Thank you for your purchase and I hope you enjoy the material.

Stephen Hoover

August of 2013

Chapter 1

BIOGRAPHIES

Stephen Hoover – Always kind to his superiors, Stephen is the first to admit you're wrong. From his humble beginnings in Humble Beginnings, Nebraska, Stephen has spent the last few years preparing for the next few years. Hungry for enlightenment, thirsty for education, starving for knowledge, he is looking for a great restaurant.

You have to hand it to Stephen, because he's too lazy to get up and get it himself. Cynic and Romantic, Realist and Optimist, Naïve and Shrewd, Loepold and Loeb, Stephen is the first to admit you're wrong, which he said already.

Although he received no formal education, he did attend LSU. Of his appearance he says, "I'm Protestant but I look Jewish. I vote to exclude myself from the clubs I join." Give him an inch and he'll take an inch. Give him enough time, and he'll go down in history.

L.A. Laird – The poverty-stricken child of only parents, L.A. Laird is a simple, unpretentious bon vivant, a devil-may-care-man-about-town loved by millions, although people don't like him.

A multi-talented prodigy who exploded out of the Midwest like a shooting star to distinguish himself with brilliant achievements as both an actor and director, Orson Welles never met L.A. Laird who was born many years later and can't act. L.A. Laird began writing soon after taking it up, and immediately began to show a talent for taking up things. Family and friends alike were surprised with his poetical bent as it is exceedingly difficult to fix bent poeticals. L.A. Laird is now eagerly pursuing a career in screenwriting, although some day he'd like to get into modeling. It is obvious that L.A. Laird has a very promising future behind him.

Together this pair is dynamite, igniting an explosive combination of comedy combustion! Stephen Hoover and L.A. Laird are ready to take the first steps on their journey from local obscurity to national oblivion.

Chapter 2

❧

"The Voice of Buster Keaton"
(Originally Published in the Damifinos Newsletter)

Talkies created the greatest revolution in film history, and sound's effect on film comedy was no less revolutionary. Sight gags became less important. Hollywood grew, in film critic Richard Schickel's phrase "drunk with words." The stars were no longer pantomimes, but rather fast talkers like Groucho Marx and Bob Hope. W.C. Fields, who'd had a middling silent career, finally achieved prominence on screen now that his inimitable voice could be heard.

Buster Keaton is generally categorized as one of the talkie casualties. However, Keaton's problem did not stem from having a "bad" voice (as did Vilma Banky and Emil Jannings, neither of whom could speak English), but from having a voice that did not match his unique screen image.

Look at the other great silent comedians:

Raymond Griffith was the only silent comedian whose career was destroyed by the talkies. He had been injured as a young man and could not speak above a whisper. He gave up acting and became a producer at Fox.

Harry Langdon's rapid and unfortunate decline began before talkies and was due to his ego, not his voice.

Although many will argue speech made Chaplin's Tramp less universal, his genteel, somewhat bourgeois English accent suited the character well. It suggested a fallen Lord, a noble gentleman who'd been caught in a scandal back in England and had come to America to escape the consequences. Chaplin's manner was never that of a real tramp.

Harold Lloyd spoke unassumingly with a soft Midwester twang, which jibed well with his image as an all-American Boy with all-American values.

Laurel and Hardy were the only major silent comedians (W. C. Fields was never a major star in silents) to become more popular in talkies. Their voices suited them, especially Hardy's. Ollie was a Southern pseudo-aristocrat, all manners and no brains, always doing the wrong thing for all the right reasons. Laurel's voice was less important because he spoke less, but sound added a certain pathos to his crying scenes that made them all the more effective.

Buster Keaton's voice was a bass marked by a nasal twang, revealing his Midwestern origin. It makes one think of a Nebraska corn farmer. The voice just didn't go with the playboy millionaire, a steamboat captain, or a Confederate locomotive engineer. Had Keaton arrived in Hollywood in 1930 he'd have been shunted off immediately into character roles. Fortunately for us, he arrived at a time at which the technology was suited to his unique talents.

The perfect voice for Buster's character would be a cultured, Ashley Wilkes sort of Southern drawl. Despite Buster's prodigious skill with gadgets, he always seemed at odds with the modern world (unlike Lloyd, who suits it well). The ideal Buster voice would have enhanced this facet of Keaton's persona – gentlemanly, more concerned with honor than pragmatism, obsessed with values rendered archaic by the 20th century. Thanks to the magic of silent films it is left to our own imaginations to supply the voice of Buster Keaton.

(Stephen Todd Hoover and L.A. Laird are a pair of aspiring screenwriters who do more aspiring than screenwriting.)

Chapter 3

❧

"The Voice of a Generation"

Imperialist Records recently announced plans to announce the planned release of the first five albums by folk-rock legend Dave Whitman as part of its CD reissue series Dave Whitman: Folk Rock Legend, or What? In one of his last interviews John Lennon summed up Whitman's influence on the music of the 1960s by saying, "Dave Whitman was very influential on the music of the 1960s, if we're talking about the same Dave Whitman, the one who was a singer and wrote songs." Whitman spoke for an entire generation when he said, "I speak for no one." Believed to be the first rock performer to smash his guitar to pieces on stage (though not on purpose), millions were to follow his lead of nonconformity. His lyrics were witty and romantic, personal and protesting, with an artistry and insight which placed him far above less gifted contemporaries such as Nelson Rockefeller.

For years Dave Whitman's early life has been shrouded in mystery, but the basic facts as we know them are these. He was born David Robert Uberman to Mr. and Mrs. Sam Uberman on May 21, 1941 in a small wooden shack located just inside his parent's mansion. Jewish, though only on his parent's side, David felt out of place in the predominantly Midwestern town of Caribou Hemorrhoids, Minnesota. One of five only children, David Uberman grew up shy and withdrawn; he was later characterized by those close to him as 'hard to get close to.'

Dave became even more of a loner after a childhood bout with mumps, which had the tragic and unexpected side effect of changing his name from "David Uberman" to "Walt Whitman." Specialists from the Mayo Clinic in nearby Rochester were called in but were only able to change his first name back to "Dave." Whitman's parent's regarded this as the will of God and immediately changed the monograms on his shirts. From this point he would be known only as Dave Whitman (though it is rumored that fraternity brothers at the University of Minnesota later briefly changed his name to Stella Adler as a college prank).

Music was Dave's one passion and his tastes were wide-ranging. He collected records by such diverse artists as The Premature Anti-Fascist Folk Quartet, (which for some reason had only three members) country singer Hank Beerhole, and legendary blues guitarist Blind Ramblin' Watch Out I Can't See Where I'm Goin'. And when rock and roll hit America in 1955 (it had meant to hit America in 1954, but its aim was bad and America kept ducking)

Dave started a rock group of his own, although his shyness kept him from recruiting any other members.

After a fairly uneventful year of college in Minneapolis, Whitman headed for the Mecca of folksingers – Mecca. As a non-believer though he was refused entry to the holy city, but he was allowed to ride a two-hump camel and travel the outskirts of town asking the pilgrims, "Hey Jack, which way to Mecca?"

Eventually Dave decided to go to New York and seek his future there. New York, 1960. It was the New York of folksingers, and was conducting negotiations to become the Mecca. Whitman naturally gravitated to the bohemian scene of Greenwich Village and scrounged for what work he could get. He was fired from one gig for taking to many coffee breaks, despite the fact that it was a coffeehouse.

The highlight of this period was when Dave saw Woody Guthrie, the father of folk music, then seriously ill and confined to his hospital room. Every folk singer in the New York area has seen Guthrie and he had not improved. Following a consultation with The Kingston Trio his condition had stabilized. Whitman saw Guthrie and recommended surgery. Guthrie's family was against such a complicated procedure – an earlier operation performed by Joan Baez has been unsuccessful. Tragically, the invalid Guthrie would never again leave his hospital bed, especially after Pete Seeger examined him and prescribed rest.

By 1961 Whitman's name was becoming well known on the New York folk circuit. His guitar work was reminiscent of Leadbelly and Jimmie Rodgers; he also played a blues-influence mouth harp, although his lips kept getting caught in the strings and he soon switched to the harmonica. Around this time Dave met the itinerant folk minstrel Ed the Tambourine Man, who would later inspire one of the Whitman's most touching compositions, "Mr. Ed."

At the end of 1961 Whitman was offered a record contract by the celebrated talent scout John "Buddy" Folly. Buddy (as "Buddy" was known) had earlier discovered Benny Goodman and Billie Holiday at the Plaza, and said he would keep quiet about it if they signed contracts with him. This established Folly at Imperialist Records, but recently there had been whispers that Folly had lost his ability to spot talent, especially after he failed to protect Roberto Clemente allowing him to be claimed by the Pirates. Folly regarded Whitman as the way to re-establish himself as an impresario.

Whitman achieved widespread anonymity in mid-1962 with the release of his debut album, A Majority of None. After its disappointing commercial performance it was re-titled How to Make Millions in Real Estate in an effort to boost sales. Most of the songs were folk standards: "Talkin' Stock Market Crash Blues", "Talkin' Depression Blues", "Talkin' Hooverville Blues", "Talkin' WPA Blues", and "Talkin' a Slight Increase in Market Production Which Failed to Resuscitate the Lagging Economy Blues". Also included was a Whitman original, an allegory about prehistoric man first discovering ice told in terms of his producer's organ playing entitled "Folly's Hammond". A Majority of None was well-received by critics. Unfortunately, after the critics received the album they listened to it and hated it. Majority broke further new ground as the first folk album simultaneously released in sign language.

In early 1963 Imperialist released Whitman's second album, The Freeloadin' Dave Whitman. His most protest-oriented record, Feeloadin' established Whitman with the burgeoning new left movement via such powerful political statements as "Shoot the Bull" (an attack on the brutal Mississippi Sheriff T. B. "Bull" Sheets, who harassed civil rights workers by checking out non-circulating reference books on their library cards) and "Why Should I Pay If It's Free?" (a tribute to the Chattanooga Seven – a group arrested after picketing for more air gauges at Texaco stations), which became a number-one pop hit when recorded by Peter, Paul, and Mary who were then, owing to a contractual dispute over billing, known as Peter, Paul, Mary, Mary, Paul, Paul, Peter, Peter, and Peter.

As a result of Whitman's growing notoriety he was invited to appear on the era's major television showcase, The Ed Sullivan Show. Whitman announced his intention to sing his composition "Talkin' Unfinished Furniture Blues". Sullivan agreed, but a CBS censor claimed it would create too much controversy within the unfinished furniture industry and banned it. Sullivan suggested that Whitman rewrite his lyrics to deal with finished furniture, or at least furniture that had been varnished. Whitman refused to allow any tampering with his work and did not do the program. As a result he would not appear on network television until a late '60s guest spot playing the title role in Black Perspective on the News.

The turning point in Dave's career came in 1964 when he abandoned the protest song for a more probing personal style. He explored the dichotomy of his own emotions on his third album, The Two-Faced Dave Whitman. His elliptical lyricism in songs such as "Elliptical Lyricism" impressed many with his oblique romanticism and unconventional use of the semi-colon. Whitman was never comfortable being called a poet (he was also never comfortable being called Chicken Lips, but he was given the name by an aunt and it stuck). Whitman had fashioned a new persona taking his politics from Guthrie, his look from James Dead, and his harmonica from Ernie's Pawn Shop on 23rd Street.

Whitman surprised his following yet again when he embraced rock and roll on his 1965 album Coppin' the Blues. Folk purists were outraged by his inclusion of amplified backing instruments such as electric spoons. Teenage America, however, was wildly enthusiastic for the new hybrid sound dubbed "folk-rock" making the album a million seller. The new record gave Whitman a smash hit single, "You're Not Going to Wear Plaid Pants with a Plaid Shirt, Are You?" which became an anthem for his generation, although the follow-up "Anthem For My Generation" flopped.

In the summer of 1965 Whitman appeared at the Shreveport Folk Festival and was booed off the stage partly because he had gone electric but mostly because he had not been invited and had sneaked in through a back gate without paying. However, the incident did not affect Whitman's popularity with rock audiences and when his fifth album, Emotion Sickness, was released in the spring of '66 it shot straight to the top of the charts like a, well, let's say, bullet. Whitman was never comfortable with being called a popular artist. Fortunately no one ever called him that, so it was never much of a problem. Tragically, a few days before the album's release, Whitman was seriously injured in a motorcycle collision when some overzealous folk purists ran over him with a motorcycle.

Whitman convalesced for over a year. He fought occasional bouts of depression, coming out of them just long enough to attempt suicide. He made other albums after his recovery but none of them equaled his earlier commercial impact, possibly because they were released only in Pakistan. He did achieve a reputation as a concert performer, his finest hour coming at 1967's Monterey Pop Festival, which he did not attend. This set the stage for Whitman's legendary non-appearance at Woodstock in 1969. By the time Whitman didn't show up at Altamont later that year, his reputation was assured.

But that cannot lessen Dave Whitman's achievements of the 1960's. His songs expressed the hopes and desires of the sixties in ways earlier singers could not because the sixties hadn't happened yet. Truly, Dave Whitman was The Voice of a Generation.

Chapter 4

❧

"Help Yourself"

ANNOUNCER
Are you unsatisfied with your life?

SHOT – Stock photo of an assembly line at an auto plant in the thirties.

ANNOUNCER (CTD)
Is your financial future bleak?

SHOT – Life Magazine Photo of Depression-era Woman.

                    ANNOUNCER (CTD)
            Do you suffer from low self esteem?

SHOT – Stock still of pilgrim being burned at the stake by Indians.

                    ANNOUNCER (CTD)
            Are your personal relationships
            unfulfilling?

SHOT – Gladiator in combat in the Arena.

                    ANNOUNCER (CTD)
            Do you feel your entire existence is a
            wretched an pathetic excuse for human
            life?

SHOT – Dan Quayle

                    ANNOUNCER (CTD)
            If so, you're probably right. But you
            don't have to let all that keep you from
            reaching your full potential. I, too, was
            once snake-eyes in the crap shoot of life,
            discouraged, and disappointed by trials
            and tribulations, dejected and anguished
            by agonizing frustrations, despondent
            and miserable from the .ordeal of
            constant defeat! But I discovered a set of
            guiding principles which enabled me to
            surmount these obstacles and achieve the
            American dream – getting on cable tv at
            3 o'clock in the morning. Yes, my name
            is F. Harve Swindelle and I'm here to
            offer you the chance to make your
            dreams come true. With my new seminar
            –

CAMERA PULLS BACK. On the table in front of him we SEE
videotapes and cassettes.

                    SWINDELLE
            "Making an Asset Out of Yourself", an
            invaluable program which can enrich

your life, you can become a winner. Just
listen to these unsolicited testimonials.

SHOT – Woman happy with her life.

> HAPPY WOMAN
> Before I took the F. Harve Swindelle
> seminar I was a drab housewife, today I
> am a well-to-do auto upholsterer.

SHOT – Expressionless man

> EXPRESSIONLESS MAN
> Before I took F. Harve Swindelle's
> seminar I didn't have a cent to my name.
> Today, I have a cent to my name.

SHOT – Businessman inside factory office

> BUSINESSMAN
> I used to be trapped in a dead-end job.
> Now, thanks to F. Harve Swindelle, I am
> a successful industrial type guy.

SHOT – Filthy newspapers, clothing, and food containers strewn
everywhere. Depressed guy lying on the bed, out of it.

> DEPRESSED GUY
> (slow, pathetic, listless)
> I was once discouraged, disappointed,
> dejected, anguished, despondent, and
> miserable. Today, thanks to F. Harve
> Swindelle, I am realizing my full
> potential.

SHOT - SWINDELLE

> SWINDELLE
> Whether you want to learn how to cope
> with stress, meet interesting people,
> make a career change, or, if you prefer,
> find meaning to your life, the Swindelle
> Seminar is for you. By calling our
> operators…

Phone # appears on screen 1-800-4HERNIA.

                          SWINDELLE
             …you can receive for the special low
             price of 39.95 these study audio cassettes
             ready to be played at home, at school, or
             in the car. Also, for the low, low price of
             79.95 you can get this videotape,
             guaranteed to be twice as effective as my
             audio cassettes. For those of you who
             want something even more effective than
             video, there is real life. The F. Harve
                       SWINDELLE (CTD)
             Swindelle "Making an Asset Out of
             Yourself" seminar will be appearing at a
             hotel or motel near you.

                          NARRATOR
             Order now by sending cash or money
             order to F. Harve Swindelle, Governor's
             Work-Release Program, Angola,
             Louisiana. Results guaranteed, but don't
             expect miracles. Sales will be limited to
             however many people buy it.

                                                    FADE OUT.

Chapter 5

~❧~

"No Inn at the Room"

Much has been written about the celebrated Al Conklin Round Table. As none of it has ever been read, however, it is hoped that this brief introduction to its history might serve as a brief introduction to its history.

Named after the famous designer of shag doormats, the Al Conklin Hotel opened its doors in 1912. As it was not ready for business until 1915 this action seems, in retrospect, to have been premature, leading to the unfortunate ransacking of the kitchen and the soiling of at least one carpet.

When Phil N. DeBlanques took over the hotel shortly after the Armistice, a new era was clearly at hand. America had stepped out of the war and into a dry martini.

Wilson was in the White House and as he had been dead for two years many pundits questioned the policy of leaving the body in the West Wing as a tourist attraction.

It was the Era of Wonderful Nonsense. Prohibition couldn't stop the good times from flowing freely, although it became very difficult to get a drink. The nation turned its eye to a Vermont Yankee, winked its eye at Babe Ruth, blinked uncontrollably at flapper Joan Crawford, and stared catatonically at a poster for furnace installation until somebody realized it was upside down. It was the best of times, it was the worst of times – it was the Twenties. However, when DeBlanques burned down the Al Conklin Hotel for the insurance money in 1919, he left the hotel's future as a gathering place for Newark's most brilliant minds somewhat in doubt.

It was Alexander Sideswipe who saw the way to the future. As drama editor of The Newark Times, Sideswipe first dined at the Cloak Room on the night of the great fire. Although he complained that his steaks were overdone, he did not otherwise feel that his evening had been impinged upon.

Sideswipe, a rotund slob, had been the toast of Passaic until moving to become the omelet with bacon on the side of Newark. Shortly after the Conklin fire, he and fellow staffer C.P.A., writer of the much read column "People Send in Great Stuff to My Office and All I Have to Do is Show Up for a Couple of Hours a Day and Paste it Together and Take All the Credit," made the hotel an institution for wayward writers and wits. Among those present included newspapermen, poets, actors, playwrights, busboys, dishwashers, a chambermaid, and Eugene O'Neill who had given his cab driver the wrong address.

There was Irwin Gaunt, the critic, playwright, and critic again when his plays flopped. Frances Meade, a gruntled employee of The Newark Times fashion department, was the only female in the group and the only one to marry homosexuals. Next to her, though crouching a bit, was Richard Stagger, the Harvard grad who had given up his dream to become a great actor in order to become a lousy actor. There was Oboe Smith, the only speaking member of the famous Smith Brothers comedy team. As he did not speak English, this severely cut into the team's booking opportunities. At the outbreak of World War II he protested against the Axis powers by changing his middle name from Adolph to Benito. Completing the circle was Frank Hooey who, once described as looking like "an assassinated Abraham Lincoln," was editing Jury and hoping to one day found a magazine of his own entitled The Newarker.

Sideswipe suggested the site of the now-defunct Conklin Hotel Cloak Room as the perfect place for a gathering of wits. Their future remarks have become too well known to repeat here. However, we will repeat them here as we have a great deal of space to fill up.

Many of Gaunt's sayings are now standards in the theater world. He once reflected, "Satire is what closes on Saturday night. Melodrama is what closes on Saturday night. All my plays seem to close on Saturday night."

At a performance of Mangoes, Gaunt stopped his backstage conversation, "Wait, I think I just heard of one of my original lines." A moment of complete silence was heard, "Yeah, that's one of mine." He also once noted, "Plays are not written, they're stolen."

About the lay A Dog's Life in the Cat's Pajamas, which continued to be a huge success despite criticism of it from the group, Gaunt wrote that it was "a bad play saved by a bad review."

Stagger once approached a man in front of the hotel wearing a tasseled costume, "Get me a taxi." He was answered, "I, sir, am a Doorman." "Okay, then get me a hotel," was his response.

Ever the world traveler, Stagger once sent a wire back to the group from Shanghai, "STREETS FULL OF CHINESE. PLEASE ADVISE."

Two ladies were discussing a proper way to take the life of a feline family pet. Meade, overhearing, remarked, "Have you tried putting it in a microwave?" (The inclusion of the word "microwave" leads the editors to believe that this story is possibly apocryphal).

On another occasion, when asked, "Have you heard Calvin Coolidge is dead?" Meade responded, "Dead?! Our President is dead?!" She then ran screaming from the room in order to attempt suicide by seeing one of Gaunt's plays.

Sideswipe once quipped on the procrastination of a friend that, "Charles Dickens, dead, writes more than William Thackeray, dead." After Stagger and Sideswipe had just finished a swim, Stagger quipped, "Let me get out of my wet clothes and into your wet clothes."

Upon seeing crowds of people in downtown Newark, Gaunt's sister remarked, "All of Rochester must be in Newark." Gaunt philosophized, "Why, what a wonderful time to visit Rochester and commit barbaric acts of pillage and raping."

But soon punchlines were replaced by bread lines. With the coming of the Depression and worldwide strife, the carrying on of the group seemed out of place, childish, and somewhat sissy. Members went off to launch unsuccessful careers of their own. Gaunt went back to his work as a critic and for many years a bad notice from him was the kiss of life to a play. Stagger gave up acting to pursue a career on the stage.

Meade made several more attempts on her life. Once, she put her head in an oven and turned on the gas, only to discover it was a microwave, and that the cat she'd placed in it had given birth to kittens.

Sideswipe became a celebrity when the Smith Brothers cast him in their play, The Man We Wrote the Play About. The play closed, however, shortly after Gaunt gave it a good review.

What brought these disparate artists together? The random chance of an arbitrary universe. What became of the home to these bon mots? It's a sad sight, but should you venture to Newark you will find that the rubble of the hotel has now been replaced by a great public building. Thus, long after the so-called wits of later generations have been forgotten, the Al Conklin Round Table will be older and even more obscure.

Chapter 6

"My Story: A Memoir"

(The editors are proud to present excerpts from the soon-to-be unpublished autobiography of British actor Oliver Tweed, who was a Hollywood star for very nearly several years.)

In 1934, I was a young actor playing Bottom to Jessica Tandy's Disgust in repertory at Forchester (pronounced "Foster") in the English Midlands when the company manager, Ronald Toppingham (also pronounced "Foster" for some reason), told me an American gentleman was waiting to see me in the manager's office. I proceeded to remove my makeup and change into street clothes causing some consternation as we were in the middle of Act Two and I was still on stage.

After the police arrived, however, and I agreed to have a drink later with the Chief Superintendent, I was able to go to the manager's office and meet my American guest. He told me to call him Marvin and that his last name was spelled F-O-S-T-E-R, although he wasn't sure how to pronounce it. Marvin was a talent scout for the world-famous Sam Goldwyn (who I believe was a Hollywood producer), and he offered me a screen test in Hollywood with all expenses paid, except travel, food, and lodging.

I leapt at the offer. It had always been my fondest dream to make a career decision irresponsibly and without forethought, and financially there was no other choice. On my rep salary I was strapped for funds to support both my invalid mother and my lifelong dream of building a museum of Portuguese cheese. What money I was able to send here she only squandered on food and shelter. Perhaps in Hollywood I could make enough so that Mum could quit her night job sharpening eyebrow pencils.

***

I will never forget my first view of Hollywood!

***

After I'd been in Hollywood a few days, I was summoned for an audience with Mr. Goldwyn. Driving past the white stucco houses and palm trees, I made by way to the Goldwyn lot. He kept me waiting in the white stucco reception area for what seemed like a month, and after four weeks I was duly taken in to the mogul's office. Mr. Goldwyn stood in front of a white stucco wall amidst a clutch of palm trees and thrust a pen and paper in my face.

"A verbal contract isn't worth the paper it's printed on," he said.

I signed the paper.

"It certainly isn't," I said.

"I can tell you in two words: I'm possible."

"Er, I beg for pard-"

"We can get all the Indians we need at the reservoir. Next time I send an idiot, I go myself. Any man who goes to a psychiatrist should have his head examined."

"If you don't mind, Mr. Goldwyn, I must be going."

"It's a dog-eat-dog world, and nobody's going to eat me."

I managed to slip out of the office, but I couldn't help thinking that Goldwyn was a whole lot shrewder than he let on. I was later proven right when the contract I signed with Goldwyn for seven-fifty a week (750 what Goldwyn would decide later) allowed him to trade me to the Red Sox for Lefty Studenko. I didn't even make it out of spring training with the Red Sox, but Lefty had a very successful career in Hollywood until he was beaned by Cecil B. DeMille on the set of Samson and Delilah.

***

Gone With the Wind, Margaret Mitchell's epic novel of the Old South, was published in 1936 and eventually became and immediate best seller. David Selznick bought the rights and planned to turn it into the most lavish picture ever produced in Hollywood. I read the book and realized whoever played the heroine, Scarlett O'Hara, would become a star overnight. I went to talk to Selznick.

"David, I want to play Scarlett."

"You play Scarlett? Don't be absurd, Oliver. You're not American."

"Please, David, I know I can do it. I've been working hard on a Southern accent. 'You all cotton to some grits'"

"I don't know…"

"Just give me a chance."

It took quite a bit of pleading, but eventually Selznick gave in and let me grovel. After a bit of groveling I eventually got to test for Scarlett but unfortunately it didn't turn out very well – I was nervous – and anyway, by that time Selznick had already decided to use Vivien Leigh. However, Selznick did cast me in a supporting role as Mammy, which my Goldwyn contract forced me to play under the name Hattie McDaniel.

***

In those carefree Hollywood days, a night on the town usually involved going out. First stop was the legendary Brown Derby restaurant on Vine Street, then over to Don the Beachcomber's in Malibu for drinks. Finally, no night out in Hollywood was complete without a trip to the Coconut Grove to watch the building catch fire. I'd stop by in my asbestos tuxedo and ask the maitre d' if anything was going on.

"Anything going on, Maurice?"

"Sadly, no, Monsieur Tweed. Earlier this evening, Randolph Scott and Gary Grant were trapped in the men's room, but their burns were quite minor. Too bad you were not here last night – the wiring system failed. Patsy Kelly and Franklin Pangborn were fried to a crisp."

Maurice thoughtfully stroked his moustache (which had been signed off in a recent blaze, though he kept it in his vest pocket so it would be handy for stroking purposes).

"Try to drop by this weekend, Monsieur. Benny Goodman and his orchestra will be here. His last engagement was so spectacular that he has only recently recovered from the skin grafting."

Benny's previous visit had, indeed, been an unforgettable night. Not only had Benny's entire band been overcome by smoke inhalation, but I had even seen the divine Garbo herself shielding Arthur Treacher from falling debris and attempting to extinguish Noel Coward on one of his rare treks west.

***

While working on Traipsing Through Tripoli for Elliot Dirge, one of the most promising homosexual directors to come west from Broadway in weeks, I happened to meet one of the script writers, a rather disheveled man who told me his name was F. Scott Fitzgerald.

"I'm a big fan of yours, Mr. Tweed," he said.

"I never talk to writers."

After that, several years passed and I didn't see him for several years.

I had just finished a day's shooting on Down to the Sea in Snips at Paramount and had stopped by the Cock and Bull, a nearby bar, for a quick gin and tonic. Sitting in a booth, quietly enjoying my drink, I felt a strong slap on my back.

"Long time no see, Ollie!"

It was Fitzgerald, nursing a Scotch and baking soda.

"Uh, yes... Hello, old boy."

I saw no reason to create an unpleasant scene, so I did not protest when he sat down uninvited. "How have you been, Mr. Fitzgerald."

"Let's not be so formal."

"Oh, alright, F."

"Maybe we should be a bit more formal. Try Scott."

He finished his drink and ordered another. "Things haven't been going too well for me, Ollie. Metro dropped my option."

"What happened?"

"I simply couldn't function in the Iron Lung anymore."

The Iron Lung was the writers' building at MGM, so named by its put-upon occupants.

"It was driving me crazy, Ollie. Finally, I asked the front office if I could work at home. They said yes, so I went back to Oxford Mississippi. Then I remembered that Oxford is William Faulkner's home, not mine. And he wouldn't let me in, either. I knocked on the door, but Faulkner turned down the radio and pretended he wasn't home. I looked under the doormat for a key – nothing."

Poor Scott. I never saw him again. Later, a mutual friend told me that the Battle of New Orleans was fought two weeks after the War of 1812 had ended, although I never did find out what happened to Fitzgerald.

(At the outbreak of World War II, Tweed was told he could best serve his country by staying in Hollywood and making films, rather than return to England and join the army. He was told this by his barber – he felt it would be presumptuous to contact a representative of the British government. After Tweed's career in motion pictures waned he spent many years on the Broadway stage, hiding behind the curtains and humming "The Man I Love" whenever the theaters were closed. Upon his mother's untimely death in a freak carbon paper accident perennial bachelor Tweed was left without any living relatives, although he was later mysteriously killed at a family reunion.)

Chapter 7

❧

THE TIME MACHINE

"THE TIME MACHINE SKETCH"

INT. SCIENCE LAB - DAY

RAYMOND ELLIOT, science reporter, is holding a microphone. Sitting next to him is FIELDING STURDLEY, inventor, wearing a white lab coat.

> RAYMOND
> Welcome to the "World of Science Report. I'm Raymond Elliott. Tonight we

introduce you to a man who has invented
a time machine. His name is Fielding
Sturdley. Is that true, sir?

STURDLEY
Yes. It's true. My name is Fielding
Sturdley.

RAYMOND
And you, sir, have invented a time machine?

STURDLEY
Yes.

RAYMOND
Is it safe to call it amazing?

STURDLEY
Well, yes, it's fairly amazing.

RAYMOND
And how long have you been working on
this amazing new invention?

STURDLEY
I'm not sure exactly. I don't have any
clocks in my house.

RAYMOND
Still, it's a very amazing machine. Think
of all of the great events in history we
can witness. The great historical figures
we can meet.

STURDLEY
I'm sorry. That's not possible with this
particular time machine because it only
goes forward. It cannot go back.

RAYMOND
Oh. So if a volunteer traveled in your
machine and went into the future, how
would he be able to return?

STURDLEY
We haven't quite figured that out yet.
That might be why we haven't gotten
many volunteers.

RAYMOND
Still, future cures in medicine, future
civi-lizations, the evolution of our planet
-- it is still amazing.

STURDLEY
Yes, amazing is the precise word for it,
yes.

RAYMOND
Are there any risks involved with time
travel, Doctor?

STURDLEY
A traveler must remember not to
interfere with the civilization that he
finds. This is known as the first rule of
time travel. So far it's the only rule of
time travel, but I'm sure we'll come up
with others.

RAYMOND
So. Where is this amazing time machine
invention?

STURDLEY
You're sitting on it.

RAYMOND
This is it? Why it looks like an ordinary
chair.

STURDLEY
Thank you.

RAYMOND
I can't tell it from any other chair.

STURDLEY
We did that so that it wouldn't frighten
our friends in the future.

RAYMOND
I see. Doctor, have you received a patent
yet on this invention?

STURDLEY
A patent? What's that?

RAYMOND
A patent. A legal designation that you are
the time machine's inventor? It entitles
you to future royalties and payments for
the invention?

STURDLEY
Good idea. I'll have to have our research
department look into that.

RAYMOND
Research it, you mean?

STURDLEY
Yes, I guess you could say that.

RAYMOND
How have you tested the time machine,
Doctor?

STURDLEY
By using it.

RAYMOND
So you yourself have traveled into the
future?

STURDLEY
No, we still use inanimate objects. We
don't want to put any lives at stake
foolishly.

RAYMOND
Can we, along with our viewers in the
public audience, witness a demonstration
of this amazing time machine?

STURDLEY
Yes, of course. I thought that was the
whole point. So, we will perform it on
this authentic 1978 Reggie Jackson
action figure.

RAYMOND
Excellent. How exciting!

STURDLEY
Wait for it. Okay. That's it!

RAYMOND
Doctor, I don't see any difference.

STURDLEY
Remember, this action figure is
experiencing everything just two seconds
before we are.

RAYMOND
Two seconds?

STURDLEY
Correct. My time machine, which I have
invented, can send a passenger precisely
two seconds into the future.

RAYMOND
But Doctor we still see the doll --

STURDLEY
Action figure.

RAYMOND
Action figure -- in front of us. And it
never disappears.

                    STURDLEY
That's a common misconception among
those not familiar with time travel. That's
the residue-effect whereby the object
projected into the future leaves a residual
image.

                    RAYMOND
And how long does the image last,
Doctor?

                    STURDLEY
Usually about two seconds.

                    RAYMOND
Two seconds. What practical functions
do you see for this invention, Doctor?

                    STURDLEY
At the present time, none.

                    RAYMOND
Doctor, is there any scientific way we
can verify that you've, in fact, broken the
time barrier?

                    STURDLEY
Just wait two seconds.

                    RAYMOND
Is there any other way, Doctor?

                    STURDLEY
You'll have to take my word for it.

                    RAYMOND
Well. That's all tonight for the World of
Science Report. I'm Raymond Elliot. Be
sure to join us next week, when we'll
meet a good Samaritan who helps the
underprivileged by secretly rotating their
tires.

                    STURDLEY
Perhaps you'd like another
demonstration?

RAYMOND
I'm sorry, Doctor. We're out of time.

STURDLEY
Do you need two seconds? I could give
them to you. The-oretically the show
could go on forever.

RAYMOND
It feels like it already has.

FADE OUT

Chapter 8

"Great Moments of Silence"

NARRATOR

Slime-Rife Records, in association with the history department at Oral Roberts University, proudly presents a priceless panorama of pages from a politically powerful past period: Great Moments of Silence. Years of research at the Bunkie Public Library and consultation with some of the tallest public officials who own emus has produced an unprecedented document of the modern era. How many of you remember this great moment of silence from John. F. Kennedy's funeral?

Five seconds of silence.

> NARRATOR
> Or this great moment of silence from the
> funeral of Robert F. Kennedy?

Five seconds of silence.

> NARRATOR
> Or this from the funeral of Senator
> Edward Kenned- oh, he's not dead yet?
> Every great funeral has a great moment
> of silence, and they're all yours with this
> lavishly produced set. Order today and
> about every other month, actually closer
> to every 52.9 days, you'll receive, in the
> mail, a classic moment of silence like
> this one.

Five seconds of silence.

> NARRATOR
> Did you recognize that? Yes, it was the
> 1965 laying to rest of Britain's most
> beloved Prime Minister Winston
> Churchill. That and other great moments
> can be found on this magnificent
> collection, guaranteed by the Bradford
> Exchange to increase in value unless it
> goes down. Recall with me now the
> sleepy streets of Paris in 1970 as French
> men and women bury Charles Degaulle
> their indefaggotable … indefaboggotle…
> infedabbable… inde -- who put this in
> the script? Their unbeatable leader.
> Listen as a hush falls over the crowd.

Five seconds of silence.

                    NARRATOR
    "Great Moments of Silence" can be
    yours simply by sending 9.95. Plus
    postage and handling to "Great Moments
    of Silence, Slime-Rife Building, Behind
    the Dog and Cat Cemetary, Mamou.
    Specify cd, cassette, or 8 track. You may
    cancel at any time as long as you keep
    paying. "Great Moments of Silence" is
    educational for the young people and
    makes a great Christmas gift. So, order
    now and you'll be able to enjoy great
    moments of silence like this 1945 classic
    for the funeral of President Roosevelt.

Seven seconds of silence.

                    NARRATOR
    Uh, it's over now.

Chapter 9

A Fugitive Must Run

FADE IN:

EXT. COUNTRY BACK ROAD – DAY

RICHARD KIMBLE (40), closely cut hair, intense eyes, runs along side a back road.

> NARRATOR (V.O.)
> The name -- Dr. Richard Kimble.
> Occupation --Fugitive from justice.
> Wrongly convicted of his wife's murder,
> he escaped in a train wreck

INSERT SHOT -- STOCK FOOTAGE of train wreck.

> NARRATOR (V.O.)
> Like that one -- on his way to Death
> Row.

BACK to SHOT.

> NARRATOR (V.O.)
> Richard Kimble is now a fugitive and he
> must run. Run to escape the police
> lieutenant obsessed with his capture. Run
> in search of his wife's killer, the One
> Headed Man. Run because running
> provides a cardiovascular workout,
> though of excellent
> course should not be considered a
> substitute for a healthy diet low in both
> fat and calories. Tonight's episode -- "A
> Fugitive Must Run."

INSERT TITLE -- "A Fugitive Must Run."

EXT. BACK ROADS -- DAY

Kimble runs:
—through the woods
—down a dirt road,
--a deserted railroad track.

> NARRATOR (V.O.)
> Richard Kimble is on the run, cold, tired,
> hungry, trapped in a man's body...

Kimble in distance runs to camera. He comes to camera, covering lens with his chest, knocking over Cameraman.

Kimble's back as he runs from now upside down camera.

> NARRATOR (V.O.)
> Always alone, he finds safety only in
> suspicion, security only in solitude.

Kimble in deserted railroad yard, lurking about.

> NARRATOR (V.O.)
> Sometimes, in his quest for the one-
> headed man, Richard Kimble is
> inexorably drawn to the city.

Kimble face is intense. Pulling back we see him in a crowd of people.

> NARRATOR (V.O.)
> But he must always remain distant, he
> must lose himself in the crowd, but never
> become part of the crowd. He must be
> one more drop in an ocean of faces.

Kimble's feet walking down crowded sidewalk.

> NARRATOR (V.O.)
> Richard Kimble must walk down the city
> streets, where the unknown is only a foot
> step away.

Kimble's feet walk down sidewalk, as other people's feet shuffle along. Towards Kimble comes Sasquatch's Bigfeet, on their merry way.

KIMBLE's feet turn around, as if to do a bipodal "take," then go back to walking.

> NARRATOR (V.O.)
> And where danger lurks behind every
> corner.

EXT. CITY STREET - NIGHT

ECU on NEWSBOY.
Read all about it!

> NEWSBOY
> Get your paper here!

PULL BACK TO REVEAL NEWSBOY holding paper, with headline reading:

"CONVICTED KILLER KIMBLE AT LARGE IN BIG IMPERSONAL CITY."

Kimble's photograph is next to the headline.

> NEWSBOY
> Escaped murderer at large! Get your
> paper here!

Kimble rounds corner, hears Newsboy, and docks into alley. Attempting to disguise himself, he dons sunglasses.

> NEWSBOY
> EXTRA! EXTRA!

Newsboy holds up another paper with headline reading:"KIMBLE NOW BELIEVED WEARING SUNGLASSES."

Kimble's photo has him wearing shades, too.

> NEWSBOY
> Kimble now believed wearing
> sunglasses! Extra! Extra!

Kimble recoils at this strange turn of events, throws down his shades and runs down the alley toward the camera.

INT. INDIANA STATE POLICE HEADQUARTERS -- DAY

CU of KIMBLE'S photo on Wanted Poster. PULL BACK TO

REVEAL LT.PHILIP GIRARD staring down at poster on bulletin board.

                    GIRARD
            (Reading from poster)
Wanted for murder. Richard Kimble,
alias Don Sherman, alias Paul Mason,
alias The Fifth Beatle.

CAPTAIN enters.

                    CAPTAIN
Still on the Kimble case, Lieutenant
Girard?

                    GIRARD
It's still an open case, Captain. It won't
be closed until Richard Kimble is
brought to justice.

                    CAPTAIN
            (Sympathetically)
Stop blaming yourself for Kimble
escaping. Just because he was in your
custody and you were guarding him.

                    GIRARD
He was my prisoner. And I'll bring in
him. I'll bring him in no matter how
many people help him. It's easy for him.
He's a convicted murderer who escaped
Death Row. Why shouldn't people trust
him?

In background we SEE map of Indiana -- in the shape of Texas.

                    GIRARD
I'm just a legally appointed officer of the
law. Nobody trusts me.

                    CAPTAIN
Maybe people trust Kimble because of
what he said at his trial. Remember?

                    GIRARD
                 (Searching)
I vaguely recall Kimble saying
something about being...innocent.

                    CAPTAIN
And that hasn't changed your mind?

                    GIRARD
I won't let it change my mind. Because
I'm an officer of the law. When an
innocent man is wrongly convicted of
murder, it's my job to see he's brought in
and executed.

                                        DISSOLVE TO:

EXT. DOWNTOWN STREET -- DAY
CU of Kimble's photo on Wanted Poster. PULL BACK TO REVEAL
GIRARD showing poster to man.

                    NARRATOR (V.O.)
And so Philip Girard searches for Richard Kimble.

SHOTS of Girdard showing Kimble's Wanted Poster to other people.
                    NARRATOR (V.O.)
Two men drawn together by Fate. One,
purser...Girard walks purposefully down
city street.

                                        DISSOLVE TO:
EXT. DOWNTOWN STREET -- DAY
Kimble walks warily down city street.

                    NARRATOR (V.O.)
The other, pursued. Kimble walks away
from camera, into distance.

                    NARRATOR (V.O.)
But even on the run, a fugitive must live.
Kimble walks into store with sign in
window reading, "HELP WANTED."

NARRATOR (V.O.)
A fugitive must take a certain kind of job
.Kimble sweeps up a store.

NARRATOR (V.O.)
The kind where no questions are
asked...Kimble flips burgers at greasy
spoon.

NARRATOR (V.O.)
...and where no experience is required.

STOCK FOOTAGE of symphony orchestra. SHOT of Kimble in
tuxedo, conducting.

NARRATOR (V.O.)
A fugitive must blend in. Kimble, in
wrinkled suit, stands in gym with four
black youths in basketball uniforms. The
five of them perform a Globetrotters-
style routine (with "Sweet Georgia
Brown" playing on soundtrack),then
Kimble sinks a layup.

NARRATOR (V.O.)
He must never draw attention to himself.

INT. STRIP CLUB -- DAY
Kimble, in wrinkled suit, is on stage performing, wrapped around a pole.

EXT. HIGHWAY -- DAY
Kimble thumbs a ride.

NARRATOR (V.O.)
He must not stay too long in one place. Car pulls up alongside Kimble.
Kimble moves to get in when car pulls away a hundred feet or so, then
stops. Passengers laugh. Kimble runs to car.

CUT TO:

SHOTS OF LT. GIRARD driving car, riding city bus. STOCK
FOOTAGE of airplane in flight. SHOT of LT. GIRARD in airplane
seat.

NARRATOR (V.O.)
For never far away is Lieutenant Girard.
Always in pursuit...

EXT. HIGHWAY -- DAY
Kimble is still chasing that car, which keeps stopping and driving off.

NARRATOR (V.O.)
Always on the trail of his quarry.

STOCK FOOTAGE of ocean liner on high seas.

NARRATOR (V.O.)(Cont'd)
In a hunt that will end only when Richard
Kimble is on Death Row.

SHOT of LT. GIRARD in deck chair, reading "OBSESSED
WITHRECAPTURING FUGITIVES MAGAZINE."

DISSOLVE TO:

INT. INDIANA STATE POLICE HEADQUARTERS -- DAY
Girard examines U.S. map. Captain enters.

CAPTAIN
Lieutenant Girard, I think you're spending too much
time and money on the Kimble case.

GIRARD
Time and money don't matter. There is
only the law.

CAPTAIN
But you're searching for Kimble in every
nook and cranny.

GIRARD
I've searched every nook, but I missed a
few crannies.

CAPTAIN
And that expense voucher you turned
in.You've traveled over three million

miles chasing Kimble this month alone.
You're the frequent flyer mileage leader
on six different airlines. When you heard
Kimble was in Hawaii you rented the
Love Boat and searched Waikiki Beach
for two weeks.

While CAPTAIN speaks, a POLICEMAN walks into background. He
sees a sign on wall reading "PLEASE TAKE ONE." POLICEMAN
studies sign, then takes sign off wall and walks away.

> CAPTAIN
> You bought ads in twelve magazines and
> commandeered time on the "Ed Sullivan
> Show" asking people if they've seen
> Kimble. And today you bought the
> Playboy Jet from Hugh Hefner. Frankly,
> Lieutenant, I'm not sure the governor
> will approve how you're spending the
> taxpayers' money.

> GIRARD
> You don't understand, Captain, I don't
> care how much it costs the taxpayers. I'll
> keep searching for Kimble until I find
> him.

Girard pounds the desk in front of him.

> GIRARD
> (Intensely)
> And when I find him, he'll be in the last
> place I look.

> CAPTAIN
> Lieutenant, just how long do you intend
> to keep after Kimble?

> GIRARD
> As long as it takes
> (To CAPTAIN)
> (Looks off into space)
> Maybe even longer.

DISSOLVE TO:

EXT. HILLSIDE -- DAY
CU on KIMBLE sweating and straining. PULL BACK TO
REVEAL KIMBLE attempting to climb steep hill.

> NARRATOR (V.O.)
> And so Richard Kimble runs. For a
> fugitive
> must run. Run to escape. Run to survive.

PULL BACK TO LONGEST SHOT POSSIBLE.

EXT. ROADSIDE -- DAY
Kimble's exhausted. Panting and sweating, he stops running.

> NARRATOR (V.O.)
> Sometimes even a fugitive must stop
> running. For a while.

Kimble walks down the road.

> NARRATOR (V.O.)
> The place -- West Virginia.

Kimble walks past a road sign reading "Welcome to Kentucky."

> NARRATOR (V.O.)
> (Confused)
> Uh... The place -- Kentucky.

Kimble walks past a sign reading "You Are Now Leaving
Kentucky."Then another reading "Welcome to West Virginia."

> NARRATOR (V.O.)
> (Annoyed)
> I was right for the first time.
> Anyway...back to pomposity). A fugitive
> must always travel back roads and hope
> he can fade into the background.

A HILLBILLY comes over to Kimble.

                    HILLBILLY
Hey, there! Yeah you, trying' to fade into the
background. Where ya from, stranger?

                    KIMBLE
Uh, out of town.

                    HILLBILLY
What do you do for a livin', boy?

                    KIMBLE
I, uh... (Stalling)

                    NARRATOR (V.O.)
When questioned, a fugitive must always
bependy to answer with a ready answer.

                    KIMBLE
I, uh, I renovate fifteenth century
Florentine architecture.

                    HILLBILLY
Ain't much call for that 'round here, boy.
Nawsir. Down here in the valley most of
us isNeo-Classicists. Course, up in the
hills there's a few Post Modernists, but
we don't much cotton to their like 'round
these parts.

SHERIFF walks into view.

                    SHERIFF
What in the name of Victor Hugo is
goin' on here?

                    HILLBILLY
Sheriff, I just caught to this suspicious
lookin' stranger trying to fade into the
background.

                    SHERIFF
                 (to KIMBLE)

We don't like suspicious lookin'
strangers trying to fade in to the
background 'round here, boy.

Kimble moves away, but Sheriff grabs him.

> SHERIFF
> You ain't goin' no place. You're coming
> home with me to meet my beautiful
> mixed up daughter. You can probably
> help her with her personal problem
> before you vanish as quickly as you
> came.

Sheriff and Kimble walk away from Hillbilly.

> SHERIFF
> You're a suspicious lookin' stranger, but
> for some reason I trust you. You wanna
> hold my wallet?

Kimble shakes his head as he and Sheriff exit frame.

> SHERIFF (O.S.)
> I have some personal letters you might
> like toread. Wanna see my diary?

INT. WEST VIRGINIA SHERIFF'S HOME -- DAY

ELLY SUE, the Sheriff'S beautiful daughter, is watching television.

> NARRATOR (O.S.)
> Tonight watch an innovative new
> dramatic series, "THE WANDERER."
> Thrill to the adventures of Dr. Robert
> Randall, an army surgeon wrongly
> convicted of murder during the Civil
> War, who escaped from a military
> stockade and now must wander the Old
> West searching for the real killer, a one-
> legged man. Tonight's episode --"A
> Wander Must Run."

Sheriff and Kimble enter.

                SHERIFF
This is my beautiful but mixed up
daughter, Elly Sue.
Elly Sue brightens up seeing the handsome stranger.

                SHERIFF
 Elly Sue, this is a suspicious lookin'
stranger I caught lurkin' in the shadows
without identification or means of
support. I think he can help you with
your personal problem before he leaves
town as mysteriously as he came.
      (To Kimble)
Well, I'll be goin' now so my daughter
can become emotionally dependent on
you.

Sheriff exits.

                KIMBLE
So, you're beautiful but mixed up.

                ELLY SUE
And you're the fugitive.

                KIMBLE
Why didn't you turn me in?

                ELLY SUE
That's not how we do things here in
Kentucky.

                KIMBLE
West Virginia.

                ELLY SUE
Yeah, that's right
      .(Realizing)
      (Back to normal)
Maybe I didn't turn you in because --I
believe you're innocent.

                            KIMBLE
                Innocent...

                                            FAST DISSOLVE TO:

INT. COURTROOM -- DAY
CU on Kimble.

                            JUDGE (O.S.)
                You stand accused of murder in the first-
                degree. How do you plead?

                            KIMBLE
                As God is my witness, I swear I'm
                innocent.

                            D.A. (O.S.)
                Objection, Your Honor.

PULL BACK TO REVEAL courtroom in shadows, with only the barest
of features. Kimble stands alone at one table, the D.A. sits at another.
The JUDGE sits behind the bench.

                            D.A.
                An improper plea has been entered.

                            JUDGE
                    (Banging gavel)
                Objection sustained. The defendant must
                plead guilty or not guilty.

                            KIMBLE
                Not guilty.

WHIP AROUND RIGHT.

The D.A. addresses the JURY (which we do not see).

                            D.A.
                The prosecution intends to prove,
                inconclusively and beyond the shadow of
                most doubts, that the defendant, Dr.
                Richard Kimble, is probably guilty. And
                if you're still not convinced, I intend to

                    D.A.(ctd)
        introduce a lot of hearsay and innuendo.
        I hope that'll do the trick.

WHIP AROUND RIGHT.

                    LADY
        in witness box. D.A. stands nearby.

                    D.A.
        Now, Madame, can you tell the jury who
        murdered Mrs. Kimble?

                    LADY
        I can say without a moment's hesitation.
            (Points to KIMBLE)
        It was probably him!

ZOOM INTO CU on KIMBLE.

CUT to ANOTHER LADY in box.

                    ANOTHER LADY
        It's absolutely horrifying, the way he
        murdered his wife. And him a doctor.
CU on KIMBLE.

CUT TO MAN in box, pointing to KIMBLE

                    MAN
        Him! He's the one!

CU on Kimble.

CUT to NUN in box.

                    NUN
        He sure looks guilty to me!

CU on Kimble.

CUT to ANOTHER MAN in box.

                         ANOTHER MAN
              I lived next door to Dr. Kimble. He was
              always so quiet. He kept pretty much to
              himself. Dr. Kimble's the last person
              you'd suspect of murdering his wife.

SHOT of Kimble half-smiling nervously.

                         ANOTHER MAN (Cont'd)
              But I guess it's always the last person
              you'd suspect.

CU on Kimble no longer smiling.

                         KIMBLE
              It's not true. I'm innocent.
                         D.A. (O.S.)
              Objection, Your Honor.

                         JUDGE
                  (Banging gavel)
              Objection sustained.

CU on Kimble from opposite angle.

                         KIMBLE
              I'm innocent. I swear I'm innocent.

PULL BACK TO REVEAL KIMBLE in witness box.

                         D.A.
                  (Bored)
              Yes, you said that.
                  (In sincerity, friendly)
              Dr. Kimble, how've you been treated
              while in police custody?

                         KIMBLE
              I can't complain. If I do, they'll beat me.

                         D.A.
              Now, Dr. Kimble, you've told the jury
              your version of what happened the night
              your wife was murdered.

(Sarcastically)
I myself found your story fascinating.
Do you
still insist your wife was murdered by a
one-
headed man?

KIMBLE
I'm innocent. It was the one-headed
man, I tell you -- the one headed man.

FAST DISSOLVE TO:

LT. GIRARD in witness box.

GIRARD
And after that diligent search, the police
could find no evidence of any one-
headed man.

D.A.
(To Judge)
Your Honor, I'd like to ask a leading
question that calls for a conclusion on the
part of the witness.

INSERT SHOT of JUDGE leaning back in chair, reading Les
Miserables.

JUDGE
Sure, go ahead.

BACK to SHOT

D.A.
Lieutenant, who do you believe killed
Mrs. Kimble?

GIRARD
All the circumstantial evidence points to
only one man.

ZOOM to CU on GIRARD Dr. Richard Kimble. GIRARD

Kimble jumps up.

                    KIMBLE
That's not true! I'm innocent.

                    D.A.
Objection, Your Honor, the defendant's
innocence is irrelevant, immaterial, and
fattening.

                    JUDGE
     (Banging gavel)
Objection sustained.

                    KIMBLE
But I'm innocent, Girard. You know it's
the truth!

                    GIRARD
I'm only interested in the law. I can't
worry about the truth.

                              WHIP AROUND RIGHT.

                    JUDGE
Ladies and Gentlemen of the jury, have
you reached a verdict?

                    FOREMAN
We have, Your Honor.(Somberly)

                    JUDGE
And how do you find the defendant?

                    FOREMAN
     (Looks at KIMBLE)
Oooooh, is he guilty.

                              WHIP AROUND RIGHT.

                    JUDGE
Richard Kimble, you have been found
guilty of murder in the first degree. Do
you have anything to say before this
court passes sentence?

> KIMBLE
> As God is my witness, I could've sworn I
> was innocent.

> JUDGE
> Richard Kimble, it is the sentence of this
> court that you be taken to an
> overcrowded prison, where, six weeks
> from today, you shall be executed at
> seven A.M. -- six Central, four Pacific.

> KIMBLE
> I'm innocent. I'm...

FAST DISSOLVE TO:

INT. SHERIFF'S HOME -- DAY

> KIMBLE
> ...innocent.

> ELLY SUE
> I believe you. More than that, I want to
> go with you!

She embraces him.

> KIMBLE
> But, you can't.

> ELLY SUE
> Why not?

> KIMBLE
> Because I'm on the run, twenty-four
> hours a day, seven days a week.
> Sometimes even longer.

> ELLY SUE
> I'll run with you. We don't have to run
> together. You can run a little ahead of
> me if you want.

> KIMBLE
> No. A fugitive must run -- alone.

He breaks free from her embrace.

> ELLY SUE
> I don't understand why you've rejected
> me. I'm more mixed up than ever.

She faints. Kimble goes to her as the Sheriff enters.

> SHERIFF
> What happened?

> KIMBLE
> Your beautiful but mixed up daughter
> fainted.

Kimble holds her as Sheriff comes over.

> KIMBLE
> Give her some air.

> SHERIFF
> Okay.

Sheriff blows in Elly Sue's face.

> KIMBLE
> Uh, that's enough air. Tell me, has your
> daughter even been sick before?

> SHERIFF
> She just had the usual childhood
> diseases. Mumps, chicken pox, Disco
> Fever...

> KIMBLE
> She's suffered an aneurysm.

Kimble recoils, realizing he's revealed his identity.

> SHERIFF
> How does a suspicious stranger like you
> know a fancy word like that...
> (Realizing)
> Hey, you ain't no drifter...you're Dr.
> Richard Kimble, the fugitive...

                    SHERIFF (ctd.)
                  (Drawing his gun)
        I trusted you when things were easy, but
        no-win a crisis, I'll show my true colors
        by turning on you.

                    KIMBLE
        Sheriff, I know that I'm a convicted
        murderer who escaped from justice on
        his way to Death Row and that I've lied
        to you from the moment we met, but
        you've got to trust me.

                    SHERIFF
          Okay.

He holsters his gun.

                    KIMBLE
        We do have plenty of time to take your
        daughter to a hospital, but if I'm going to
        operate on her it will have to be here, in
        the primitive and unsanitary conditions
        of this office.

                    SHERIFF
          Right!

Sheriff moves away. Kimble grabs him.

Sheriff exits. Kimble produces a saw and hammer and moves toward
the camera, "mad doctor" style.

                                        DISSOLVE TO:

LATER

Kimble bandages Elly Sue's head as the Sheriff watches. Girard enters
pointing a gun.

                    GIRARD
          Okay, Dr. Kimble. I've got you now. I
          intend to see you hang in the electric
          chair. Move away from that girl.

                    SHERIFF
          But he's trying to save my daughter's
          life.

                    GIRARD
          I'm an officer of The Law. I can't worry
          about people's lives.

                    KIMBLE
          I'm finished anyway.

                    SHERIFF
          How is she, Doctor?

                    KIMBLE
          I'm not sure. I had to relieve the
          pressure inside her skull. So I took out
          her brain. I've got it inside this shoe
          box.

He lifts a shoe box.

                    SHERIFF
          Will she be alright?

                    SHERIFF
          Dr. Kimble?

                    KIMBLE
          Only time will tell. Watch her for a few
          days. If there's no improvement, put her
          brain back in.

He hands the shoe box to the Sheriff.

                    GIRARD
          Okay, Kimble. Let's go. You've got a
          date with the hangman. So, be sure to
          put on some cologne.

The phone rings. Sheriff answers.

GIRARD
How do you do it, Kimble? How do you
get people to trust you?

KIMBLE
It's simple, Lieutenant...
(Whispering)
I always pick very stupid people.

SHERIFF
Lt. Girard, it's for you. It's the governor
of Indiana.

Sheriff hands phone to Girard.

GIRARD
Hello? Yes, operator, I'll accept charges.
Hello, Governor. What? You found the
One Headed Man? He confessed to
everything? Kimble is cleared? I see.
Yes. I'll belying back to Indiana,
although I may stop off in Chicago to see
Hef at the mansion. What? I am? I see,
Governor. Goodbye.

Girard hangs up the phone.

KIMBLE
I guess today -- the Running Stops.
You're running, maybe.

GIRARD
Trying to recapture you, I ended up
spending eighty seven million dollars
from the Indiana state treasury.

Girard is stunned.
GIRARD
I've been indicted for misappropriation
of funds, fraud, embezzlement,
malfeasance, misfeasance, and
nonfeasance. (Puzzled)
And for some reason, sexual harassment
(almost pleading)
.All I did was ask her out.

                    KIMBLE
               (Sympathetically)
          Women are so touchy lately.

                    GIRARD
          Well, I'm a wanted man now. Have to
          run!

                    KIMBLE
          Wait a second. You cost the state of
          Indiana 87 million dollars? Reward out
          for you. They probably have a big
          Would you mind if I became obsessed
          with your capture?

                    GIRARD
               (Gives Kimble his gun.)
          Sure, why not?

But you've got to give me a head start.

                    KIMBLE
               Okay.

Kimble closes his eyes then puts his hands over them.

                    KIMBLE
          One Mississippi, two Mississippi...

Girard exits.

EXT. BACK ROAD -- DAY
Girard jogs down a country back road.

                    NARRATOR
          Lt. Philip Girard is now a Kimble -- and
          a fugitive must run. Not walk very fast,
          but run.

Girard speeds up his pace.

                    NARRATOR (V.O.)
See the fugitive run. Run fugitive run.
Run! Run! Run! C'mon man, run!
Grandmother can run faster than that!
Speedway, my it up, slowpoke! What's a
matter, got a piano on your back? Get
the lead out! Run! Run! Run!

                                                FADE OUT.
                    THE END

Chapter 10

❦

COURTSHIP

"Nice Work if You Can Get It"

(A pilot for a three-camera sitcom with the concept "A CONFEDERACY OF DUNCES zaniness set in a New Orleans law firm." Perhaps a tad more autobiographical than I'd like the script is something of homage to the 'workplace as family' sitcoms I love such as DICK VAN DYKE SHOW, MARY TYLER MOORE SHOW, TAXI, and CHEERS.)

ACT ONE

A PICTURESQUE SECTION OF MAGAZINE STREET.

NEXT TO AN AGING BUILDING WITH OLD-WORLD CHARM IS A SIGN: "FELDON, FELDON, & FELDON, Law Firm."

INT. FELDON MAIN OFFICE - DAY

AN OPEN ROOM WITH AGING WOODEN DESKS. PAPERS, FILES, AND FOLDERS ARE STREWN ABOUT.

DRUSILLA LANDRY, MID-FORTIES, EFFICIENT, NO NONSENSE -- PURPOSEFULLY SEARCHES THROUGH ONE OF THE MANY STACKS OF FILES.

VERONICA CARLISLE, MID-TWENTIES, IMMACULATELY DRESSED IN BUSINESS ATTIRE MORE APPROPRIATE TO WALL STREET -- SHE HAS AN IMPERIOUS AIR -- IS MORE CASUAL IN HER PERUSAL OF THE FILES.

TONY MURPHY, EARLY TWENTIES, FRAT BOY GOOD LOOKS ALTHOUGH HE'S NEVER BEEN NEAR A COLLEGE (EXCEPT FOR KEG PARTIES), A LITTLE SLOW AND HARMLESS -- ALSO ASSISTS.

> DRUSILLA
> Tony, are you sure, you looked under
> "M" for McReynolds?

> TONY
> I looked. It wasn't there.

> DRUSILLA
> Maybe you filed it under "R" for
> Reynolds?

                    TONY
          I looked. It wasn't there.

                    DRUSILLA
                    (EXASPERATED)
          Why not try "D" for Disorganized
          Dumbbell?

                    TONY
          I looked. It wasn't there.

                    DRUSILLA
          I saw it yesterday. Veronica, you worked
          on the case. Don't you remember
          anything?

                    VERONICA
          I left Tulane at eleven forty-five. Had
          lunch. Vaguely considered the Portobello
          sandwich but went Pasta Alfredo. Light
          butter, extra cheese, no basil. Arrived at
          the office promptly at one p.m. Worked
          on the McReynolds file for two point
          five billable hours. Yes. I remember
          every detail.

                    DRUSILLA
          So where did you leave the file?

                    VERONICA
          Except that one.

THEY RESUME SEARCHING. VERONICA SETS DOWN A
FILE NEXT TO DRUSILLA, WHO PICKS IT UP AND LEAFS
THROUGH IT.

                    DRUSILLA
          Here it is!

VERONICA DOUBLE-TAKES, AGHAST. HER MOUTH OPENS,
BUT NO WORDS COME.

                    DRUSILLA
          Ha! Always in the last place you look.

                    TONY
          Then why didn't you look there first?

BONNIE SHARP SWEEPS INTO THE OFFICE. IN HER EARLY
TWENTIES, DRESSED IN A CASUAL SWEATER AND SKIRT.

                    DRUSILLA
          May I help you?

                    BONNIE
          Is this the office of Feldon, Feldon, and
          Feldon?

TONY LOOKS BONNIE UP AND DOWN, ATTRACTED.

                    TONY
          Yes it is. Yes it is. Yes it is.

                    BONNIE
          I'm Bonnie Sharp.

                    VERONICA
          Veronica Carlisle. Senior Law Clerk.

                    DRUSIILA
          The only law clerk.

VERONICA GLANCES AT DRUSILLA IN DISDAIN.

                    DRUSILLA
          Drusilla Landry, everybody calls me Dru.
          I'm Executive Secretary for the office.

BONNIE QUICKLY SCANS THE OFFICE.

                    BONNIE
          The only secretary for the office?

                    DRUSILLA
          Mm-mm.

                    VERONICA
          And I'm just interning here while I'm
          attending Tulane Law School.

> TONY
> What brings you here, beautiful?

> DRUSILLA
> Are you here about a case? Car wreck?
> Insurance claim?
> > (GLANCING AT TONY)
> Sexual harassment?

> BONNIE
> I'm here to join the team.

> TONY
> Nice! What's the game?

> DRUSILLA
> Tony, you're the office runner. Why
> don't you –

DRUSILLA HANDS TONY SEVERAL ENVELOPES AND
FOLDERS.

> DRUSILLA
> Run along?

DRUSILLA HUSTLES TONY OUT. SHE TURNS TO BONNIE.

> DRUSILLA
> Okay dear, let's start at the beginning.

> BONNIE
> I'm the new paralegal. I'm here to see
> Mr. Feldon. Or if he's busy I can see Mr.
> Feldon. Any of the Feldons.

> DRUSILLA
> Mr. Feldon hired you?

> BONNIE
> No, it was Danny Galliano, your Senior
> Paralegal.

> DRUSILLA
> Our only paralegal.

                    BONNIE
I met Danny when he came up to
Bogalusa, where I'm from. I just finished
paralegal school and helped on the
chemical spill case there. That's when he
offered me the job.

                    DRUSILLA
I'm afraid that Danny may have
exceeded his authority.

                    BONNIE
How?

                    VERONICA
By implying he has any. Danny Boy
doesn't do the hiring and firing around
here.

                    DRUSILLA
                    (SYMPATHETICALLY)
That's up to Mr. Feldon.

                    BONNIE
But Danny told me I had the job! I
moved here and got an apartment and
everything.

                    DRUSILLA
Mr. Feldon will be in soon and I'm sure
we can sort all this out.

DANNY   GALLIANO,   MID-THIRTIES,   LIVE-WIRE
DEALMAKER, BARGES INTO THE ROOM TALKING
LOUDLY ON HIS CELLPHONE.

                    DANNY
                    (INTO PHONE) I understand. Listen,
when we took your case I
promised you results... See? Exactly!
Losing is a result. Hello?

DANNY LOOKS AT THE PHONE, THEN TO DRUSILLA. SHAKES HIS HEAD IN DISBELIEF.

> DANNY
> Some people. Joker expected to collect just because he was dragged out of his house naked in handcuffs.

> DRUSILLA
> The cops should've at least let him get dressed.

> DANNY
> Cops? No, it was a "girl" he picked up on Bourbon Street.

DRUSILLA HANDS HIM A STACK OF MAIL.

> DRUSILLA
> Sounds like you're having a bad day.

> DANNY
> Any day I'm not subpoenaed is a great day.

> VERONICA
> (REMEMBERING)
> Oh, yeah. I almost forgot.

VERONICA HANDS DANNY SEVERAL LEGAL-SIZED PAPERS.

> VERONICA
> This came while you were out.

DANNY BRIEFLY CHECKS THEM OUT AND GRIMACES.

> DANNY
> Thanks a lot. Is Mrs. Boudreaux here?

> VERONICA
> With another one of her crazy cases?

                    DANNY
That's not fair. Only half of her cases are
crazy.

                    DRUSILLA
She's not here yet.

                    VERONICA
But our alleged new paralegal is here.

DANNY GREETS BONNIE AMIABLY.

                    DANNY
Hey, Bonnie.

                    BONNIE
I wanted to get going on my new job.

                    VERONICA
Don't worry. If it doesn't work, I'm sure
you can still get your job back at The
Mayberry Diner.

VERONICA RETURNS TO HER DESK.

                    DANNY
Don't mind her. Her family is old
money.   But they don't have money any
more. Now they're just old.

DANNY THROWS HIS PAPERS ON A NEARBY DESK.

                    BONNIE
They told me I don't have a job.

                    DRUSILLA
I don't know if we'll be able to keep her
on, Danny. (TO BONNIE) What big
cases we have are dragging on and on, no
sign of settlement. The rest are divorces,
DWI's...

                    DANNY
Yeah, it's hard to make your nut for the
year when your big moneymaker is
notarizing library card applications.

                    DRUSILLA
When Mr. Feldon comes in he can
decide.

                    VERONICA
Charles Feldon can never decide
anything. He's completely wishy washy.

                    DANNY
He can't even decide that. Some days
he's wishy -- some days he's washy.

                    VERONICA
We don't need another paralegal.

                    DANNY
We need her.

                    VERONICA
We DON'T need her.

                    DANNY
We DO need her.

AMID THIS UPROAR, CHARLIE FELDON SLIPS IN QUIETLY.
UNASSUMING, GOOD-LOOKING, LAID-BACK MAN, MID-
THIRTIES, DRESSED PROFESSIONALLY BUT NOT
SHARPLY.

FELDON HANGS UP HIS COAT ON A NEARBY RACK. HE
SEES THE GROUP IS CAUGHT UP IN A HEATED ARGUMENT
AND DOESN'T NOTICE HIM.

HE QUIETLY PUTS THE COAT BACK ON AND ATTEMPTS
TO WALK BACK OUT OF THE OFFICE UNNOTICED.

                    GROUP
              Mr. Feldon!!!

FELDON
Calm down. Calm down. I want one
person to tell me what's going on.

VERONICA
The --

FELDON
One person who isn't you.

DRUSILLA
This girl showed up saying she was
promised a paralegal job.

FELDON
(TO BONNIE)
Young lady, one thing is standing in the
way of your getting this job.

BONNIE
What's that?

FELDON
Who are you?

BONNIE
Oh, I'm Bonnie Sharp.

DANNY
She helped us out on the chemical spill
case in Bogalusa.

BONNIE
Yes sir, that's right.

DANNY
Whaddya gonna do, chief?

DRUSILLA
Why don't you just flip a coin?

BONNIE
You wouldn't decide whether to hire
someone by flipping a coin, would you?

FELDON
How do you think Veronica got here?

DRUSILLA
Mr. Feldon, I need to go over a situation
with you.

FELDON
Sorry, I have a very important deposition
to attend.

FELDON STARTS WALKING OUT THE DOOR.

DRUSILLA
That's tomorrow.

FELDON REENTERS IN ONE SMOOTH MOTION.

FELDON
Which is why I'm not going today.

DRUSILLA
Mr. Feldon, I think you and I need to talk
in your office.

FELDON ENTERS HIS PRIVATE OFFICE WITH DRUSILLA
CLOSE BEHIND. THE GROUP FOLLOWS. DRUSILLA STOPS
THEM.

DRUSILLA
(TO GROUP)
Alone.

INT. FELDON'S PRIVATE OFFICE - DAY FELDON SITS
BEHIND HIS DESK.

FELDON
What do you think?

DRUSILLA
Bonnie seems really sweet.

                    FELDON
I'm sure she loves puppies and washes
windows at the old folks home. The point
is, I don't know if I can afford to hire
another paralegal. And with this
Bogalusa case tanking-

DANNY ENTERS.

                    DANNY
I don't mean to interrupt, but –

                    FELDON
Why'd you offer that girl a job?

                    DANNY
I got a little carried away.

VERONICA ENTERS.

                    VERONICA
Excuse me, but –

                    FELDON
Yeah, we know - You don't mean to
interrupt.

                    VERONICA
No, I mean to interrupt. Why do you
think I came in here? I don't like this new
girl.

                    DANNY
That's one point in her favor.

INT. FELDON MAIN OFFICE – DAY

MRS. BOUDREAUX ENTERS. IN HER SIXTIES.

                    MRS. BOUDREAUX
                    (TO BONNIE)
Pardon me, young lady.

                    BONNIE
Yes, ma'am?

                    MRS. BOUDREAUX
I'm here for an appointment with Danny
Galliano.

                    BONNIE
He's in a meeting right now.

                    MRS. BOUDREAUX
I'm a bit late anyway. I had to take my
son-in-law in for a flea dip.

INT. FELDON'S PRIVATE OFFICE - DAY

                    DANNY
I think it's your call, chief.

                    FELDON
What a mess.

                    DRUSILLA
Talk to her. I'm sure you'll make a well-
reasoned choice.

                    FELDON
Yeah, you're right. You got a coin on
you?

                                        FADE OUT.

                    END OF ACT ONE

FADE IN:

ACT TWO

INT. FELDON MAIN OFFICE - DAY

FELDON'S PRIVATE OFFICE DOOR OPENS. DRUSILLA, DANNY, AND VERONICA LEAVE. FELDON APPEARS IN THE DOOR.

> FELDON
> Bonnie?

> BONNIE
> Yes, sir.

BONNIE WALKS OVER, WHILE DANNY GOES TO MRS. BOUDREAUX.

> DANNY
> Mrs. Boudreaux, how you doing?

MRS. BOUDREAUX FLINCHES, WHIPS OUT AN ELEGANT HAND FAN. SHE CLUTCHES DANNY'S ARM AND FANS HER FACE DRAMATICALLY.

> MRS. BOUDREAUX
> Terrible, Danny. I have an awful
> headache.

DANNY USHERS HER OVER TO HIS DESK. SHE FLUMPS BACK IN THE GUEST CHAIR.

> DANNY
> That's too bad.

> MRS. BOUDREAUX
> It's not too bad. It's an outrage! I was
> walking past Jackson Square, minding
> my own business, when I was struck by
> the sunlight shining off the statue of

Andrew Jackson. It was so bright, I went
blind!
            (RECITING BY ROTE)
It caused me pain and suffering -- yea,
much pain and suffering.

DANNY PATIENTLY SEARCHES HIS DESK FOR THE USUAL
FORMS.

                    MRS. BOUDREAUX
And-- And mental anguish! I
specifically remember,
there was a great deal of mental anguish.

MRS. BOUDREAUX BANGS HER FIST ON DANNY'S DESK.

                    MRS. BOUDREAUX
They can't treat me like this! I have my
rights! This is America!

                    DANNY
                (RESIGNED)
So, you were assaulted and traumatized
by the statue of Andrew Jackson?
                    MRS. BOUDREAUX
Precisely. And his horse.

                    DANNY
                (HUMORING HER)
And his horse. Hmmm, not sure who'd be
liable there -- who can we sue? The city?
The descendants of Andrew Jackson?
Maybe the army -- after all, he was a
general...

INT. FELDON'S PRIVATE OFFICE - DAY

BONNIE AND FELDON WALK IN. HE MOTIONS FOR HER TO
SIT DOWN.

                    FELDON
Yes, uh... I don't really know how to say
this. I'm sorry but it appears that Danny
exceeded his authority.

BONNIE
By implying he has any authority?

FELDON
(SURPRISED)
That's right.

BONNIE
Danny hired me because I helped him so
much on the Bogalusa case. I'm a
certified paralegal and --

FELDON
That's great but I just, I dunno, I just
don't think I really have a job for you
right now.

BONNIE
What about the other Feldons? Feldon,
Feldon, and Feldon?

FELDON
The fact is there aren't any other
Feldons.

BONNIE
You're the only Feldon? Then why are
there three Feldons in the firm's name?

FELDON SHRUGS.

FELDON
Meh. I just thought it would sound more
impressive if there were three of me.

BONNIE
Why did you stop with three? Why not
four? Five? Six?

FELDON
That would make the whole thing sound
phony.

BONNIE
So, you're the last of the Feldons?

                    FELDON
The last of a dying breed. I'm the one
that makes all the decisions at this firm --
All the decisions. The buck stops here.

DANNY STICKS HIS HEAD IN THE DOOR HOLDING SOME
PAPERS.

                    DANNY
                 (TO BOTH)
Excuse me.
                 (TO FELDON)
I need authorization for Mrs.
Boudreaux's medical test.

                    FELDON
Mmmmm. I dunno. You know what my
signature looks like - Why don't you go
ahead and take care of it.

DANNY EXITS.

                    BONNIE
I did bring my resume' if you'd like to
see my qualifications.

BONNIE HANDS THE RESUME' TO FELDON, WHO TAKES IT
RELUCTANTLY.

                    FELDON
So... You're from Bogalusa... I see, I
see.

                    BONNIE
Born and raised.

                    FELDON
Paralegal degree.

                    BONNIE
I took extension courses and worked all
during that time. I was a vet assistant and
worked on my family's farm.

FELDON
Law experience. Feldon, Feldon, and
Feldon?

BONNIE
That's the Bogalusa case. I helped Danny
out. I organized the entire file. That gave
me some great experience.

FELDON
You were president of your high school
3-H Club. 3-H?

BONNIE
It was a small school.

FELDON PUTS DOWN THE RESUME.

FELDON
We're not one of those big downtown
mega-firms. We care about people. We
care about our staff, but most of all we
care about our clients. At this firm the
client comes first.

DRUSILLA CRACKS THE DOOR AND NOSES INTO THE
OFFICE.

DRUSILLA
Mr. Hackford's on line one. He's been
detained again, and claims they didn't
have a warrant to search his--

FELDON
Tell him I'm not here!

DRUSILLA BACKS OUT OF THE OFFICE.

BONNIE
Too bad you couldn't have let one of the
other Feldons handle it for you.

FELDON
What I'd really rather have them do are
the job interviews.

> BONNIE
> But it's all up to you, isn't it?

> FELDON
> Danny said you work hard, and you're
> certainly qualified. But Veronica
> researched the Bogalusa case and it looks
> like a loser. I'm probably going to have
> to drop it anyway.

> BONNIE
> You can't do that. A lot of people are
> depending on that case.

> FELDON
> Litigation is expensive. It's a business
> decision.

> BONNIE
> But my own family's farm was
> contaminated.

> FELDON
> And with the Bogalusa case dead in the
> water, I really can't afford to take
> on a new paralegal.

BONNIE RISES FROM HER CHAIR.

> FELDON
> I just don't know what I can do.

INT. FELDON MAIN OFFICE - DAY

VERONICA EAVESDROPS WITH HER EAR AGAINST THE
DOOR.

> DANNY
> Why are you standing there with your ear
> pressed against the door?

VERONICA PALES.

                    VERONICA
          I...

                    DANNY
          You can hear much better with this.
DANNY PRODUCES TWO GLASSES. HE RESTS HIS AGAINST
THE DOOR AND USES IT TO LISTEN. VERONICA DOES THE
SAME. DRUSILLA WALKS OVER.

GERARD BRETAIGNE MAKES HIS WAY INTO THE OFFICE.
AROUND THE SAME AGE AS FELDON, BRETAIGNE IS
WELL-DRESSED IN BROOKS BROTHERS' LATEST.

BRETAIGNE IS UNNOTICED BY THE GROUP AS THEY
LISTEN INTENTLY AT THE DOOR.

                    BRETAIGNE
          I can see this crowd is all ears.

                    DRUSILLA
          Mr. Bretaigne.

                    BRETAIGNE
          How's it going, Dru?

                    DRUSILLA
          Mr. Feldon will be with you in a minute.
          He's in a private meeting.

                    BRETAIGNE
          No problem. I'll just pull up a glass and
          wait.

DRUSILLA WALKS AWAY FORM THE DOOR.

                    DRUSILLA
          Can I get you anything?

                    BRETAIGNE
          No, I'm fine.

                    VERONICA
Excuse me, are you Gerard Bretaigne of
Bretaigne, Norman, & Calais?

                    BRETAIGNE
If I'm not, all my stationery is misprinted.

VERONICA EXTENDS HER HAND AND THEN REALIZES
SHE'S STILL HOLDING THE GLASS. SHE NERVOUSLY
MOVES THE GLASS BEHIND HER BACK.

                    VERONICA
Veronica Carlisle. Senior law clerk.

                    BRETAIGNE
I see the office here is getting lovelier
every day.

BELIEVING THE COMPLIMENT IS FOR HER, MRS.
BOUDREAUX REACTS WITH COYISH MODESTY.

                    MRS. BOUDREAUX
Why, thank you. Just some little old
Botox treatments. I can see some people
still have manners.

BRETAIGNE REDIRECTS HIS ATTENTION BACK TO
VERONICA.

                    BRETAIGNE
Miss Carlisle --

                    VERONICA
-- Veronica.

                    BRETAIGNE
Veronica. What a lovely name.

FELDON WALKS OUT OF HIS OFFICE.

                    BRETAIGNE
Charlie!

BRETAIGNE HITS FELDON IN THE SHOULDER WITH OVERLY CHUMMY- STYLE. FELDON RUBS HIS SHOULDER IN PAIN.

> FELDON
> Gerry.

BONNIE FOLLOWS FELDON OUT OF THE OFFICE.

> BRETAIGNE
> I didn't realize you were with a client.

> BONNIE
> I was just interviewing for the paralegal job.

THEY SHAKE HANDS.

> BRETAIGNE
> The office here is getting lovelier every day.

MRS. BOUDREAUX BLUSHES.

> MRS. BOUDREAUX
> Now stop that before you make me moan with pleasure.

BONNIE AND BRETAIGNE LOOK IN MRS. BOUDREAUX'S DIRECTION, THEN RETURN TO THEIR CONVERSATION.

> BONNIE
> I don't work here.
> BRETAIGNE
> Oh?

> BONNIE
> I was interviewing for the paralegal job -- unsuccessfully.

> BRETAIGNE
> That's too bad.

BONNIE WALKS AWAY.

                    BRETAIGNE
Charlie, here's the medical report for the
driver in the Bogalusa case.

BRETAIGNE HANDS FELDON THE REPORT AND FELDON
EXAMINES IT.

                    BRETAIGNE
You couldn't beat me in moot court
back at Tulane and you're not going to
beat me now.

                    FELDON
I see you're not going to wait for the
official opening of gloating season.

                    VERONICA
I'll file that.
          (TO BRETAIGNE)
It was a Veronica Carlisle case.

VERONICA TAKES THE REPORT FROM FELDON.

FELDON AND BRETAIGNE ENTER FELDON'S PRIVATE
OFFICE. BONNIE DEJECTEDLY WALKS UP TO DANNY AND
DRUSILLA.

                    DRUSILLA
What are you going to do now?

BONNIE SHRUGS.

                    DRUSILLA
Are you going to move back home?

                    BONNIE
I don't know what I'm going to do.

                    DRUSILLA
That's a shame, honey.

                    DANNY
Was my fault.

> BONNIE
> What am I going to do for a job?

> VERONICA
> I hear they have a job opening at the
> Bogalusa bait and tackle shop. Now
> where do I file this report?

> BONNIE
> Can I see that?

> VERONICA
> Trying to make the resume' legit?

BONNIE LEAFS THROUGH THE REPORT.

> VERONICA
> That Bogalusa case is a loser anyway. I
> told Feldon the firm should drop it.

> DANNY
> Bonnie, you did a great job organizing
> this—

> BONNIE
> Hold on.

BONNIE EXAMINES EIGHT-BY-TEN PHOTOGRAPHS FROM
THE FOLDER AS FELDON AND BRETAIGNE COME OUT OF
HIS OFFICE.

> BRETAIGNE
> Might as well cut your losses, Charlie.
> This case is such a dog it has fleas and
> licks its own--

> FELDON
> I'll consider dismissing it.

> BRETAIGNE
> Losers like this are keeping you here on
> Magazine Street, instead of down on
> Poydras Avenue with me.

BONNIE
Mr. Feldon, you can't drop this suit.

FELDON
Then I'll toss it aside gently.

BONNIE
This blood alcohol test is for Dwayne
Broussard.

FELDON
Yeah, the driver of the truck that turned
over.

BONNIE
Broussard was the passenger.

BRETAIGNE
Young lady, you really aren't familiar
with the facts here--

FELDON
Wait a second, let her talk
. (TO BONNIE)
Broussard wasn't the driver?

BONNIE SHOWS THEM PHOTOGRAPHS FROM THE FOLDER.

BONNIE
If you look at the accident scene
photographs you see the position of the
seats after the crash. Broussard was tall,
about six foot five? Right?

FELDON
Right.

BONNIE
And the other guy in the truck with him,
Mark Fontenot, was about five
seven?

BRETAIGNE
Yes. So?

> BONNIE
> The truck flipped over and they both got
> out as fast as they could. The seat
> positions in the photographs.

BONNIE HOLDS UP THE PHOTOGRAPHS, POINTING OUT A
SPECIFIC SECTION TO FELDON AND BRETAIGNE.

> BONNIE
> See? The driver's seat is pushed much
> further forward than the passenger seat.
> Short stuff was driving.

BRETAIGNE SNATCHES THE PHOTOGRAPHS FROM
BONNIE AND EXAMINES THEM CLOSELY. HE NODS.
BRETAIGNE SWALLOWS NERVOUSLY, STRAIGHTENS HIS
SPINE.

> BRETAIGNE
> It would appear that my client has made
> a misstatement as to the facts.

> FELDON
> If that means he lied, yes.

> BRETAIGNE
> I'll have to have my expert look over this
> new evidence.

> FELDON
> And I'll have my expert look at it too, as
> soon as I get an expert.

DANNY AND DRUSILLA GO OVER TO BONNIE.

> DANNY
> The cavalry arrived.

> DRUSILLA
> Yeah, nice going honey.

> BONNIE
> Call it my last hurrah for the firm.

                    DRUSILLA
There must be some way to keep you
here.

BRETAIGNE APPROACHES VERONICA.

                    BRETAIGNE
By the way, if you're ever in the market
for another job I might be able to help.

VERONICA PERKS UP.

                    VERONICA
Oh?

                    BRETAIGNE
My firm might be able to use an
experienced law clerk.

                    VERONICA
I don't have much experience.

                    BRETAIGNE
I could still use you.

                    VERONICA
Maybe you could.

                    BRETAIGNE
Why don't you join me for a drink
sometime to discuss it? Our firm has
many fringe benefits.

                    VERONICA
Sounds like it might be an interesting
position.

BRETAIGNE LEAVES.

                    VERONICA
That Bretaigne is something. You have to
admire someone that successful.

                    FELDON
I worship the people he walks on.

BONNIE
Looks like the Bogalusa case is still open
-- for now.

FELDON
Yeah, I guess so. Since you're already
here and have done so much work on the
case, maybe we could take you on -- you
know, temporarily. See how it goes.

BONNIE
Before the firm makes this decision don't
you have to have a partner's meeting
with all the other Feldons?

FELDON
It's okay. I have their proxy. TONY

STROLLS INTO THE OFFICE.

TONY
I'm back! Did I miss anything?

VERONICA
Just a few millions years of evolution.

TONY
Man, I was gone longer than I thought.

FELDON
Tony, why did I hire you?

TONY SHRUGS.

TONY
Ya got me, Uncle Charlie.

DRUSILLA
Did you deliver that file?

TONY
Sure.
    (TO BONNIE; LEERING)
I always get it where it's got to go. Glad
to see you're still here.

                    BONNIE
        Just starting my new job.

                    DRUSILLA
        She's part of the firm now.

                    FELDON
        Dru, why don't you show Bonnie her
        new desk.

THEY MOVE TO BONNIE'S DESK AREA.

                    DRUSILLA
        Here's your desk over here.

                    BONNIE
        I have my very own desk.

BONNIE PROUDLY RUBS HER HAND ACROSS THE
SURFACE OF THE DESK.

                    BONNIE
        And my very own dust.

                    DRUSILLA
        Sorry about that.

                    BONNIE
        It doesn't matter. I know I'm really going
        to like being here.

                    FELDON
        We know you will.

THE GROUP IS ALL SMILES... THEN FELDON IS BACK TO
BUSINESS.

                    FELDON
        And you can start now. Draft an
        appellate brief on this McReynolds case.

BONNIE NODS AS THE SMILE ON HER FACE FADES. EVERYONE RETURNS TO THE HUSTLE AND BUSTLE OF THE FAST-PACED LEGAL WORLD.

BONNIE ROLLS HER NECK AND FACES HER MOUNTAIN OF WORK.

FADE OUT.

INT. FELDON OFFICE - NIGHT

TAG

BONNIE, ALONE IN THE DIMLY-LIT OFFICE, READS OVER A LENGTHY DEPOSITION, OCCASIONALLY JOTTING DOWN NOTES ON A YELLOW LEGAL PAD.

KEYS RATTLE AND THE FRONT OFFICE DOOR OPENS. BONNIE STANDS UP APPREHENSIVELY -- IT'S FELDON. FELDON TURNS ON THE MAIN OFFICE LIGHTS.

> BONNIE
> Oh, Mr. Feldon. I was just going over
> that file for the hearing tomorrow.

> FELDON
> You don't have to stay up here this late. I
> don't want you to turn into one of those
> workaholic drudges who spends all their
> time at the office.

> BONNIE
> What are you doing up here?

> FELDON
> I'll get the coffee.

FELDON WALKS TO THE COFFEE MAKER.

                    BONNIE
I have to learn this.   I'm in a different
world now. Everyone's been so nice and
helpful -- Danny, Dru, Tony...
          (PAINED EXPRESSION)
 Veronica.

                    FELDON
Yeah, Veronica is a bit -- enthusiastic.
She reminds me of myself when I was
that age.

FELDON STARES OFF REMEMBERING.

FELDON Man, was I a jerk.

FELDON WALKS TO HIS OFFICE DOOR.

                    FELDON
Look, I'm not very good with
compliments, but what you did here
today, it was really very... Not that bad.

                    BONNIE
 You're right.

                    FELDON
I am?

                    BONNIE
You're not very good with compliments.

FELDON LOOKS AT HER BLANKLY FOR A MOMENT, THEN
SMILES. BONNIE SMILES BACK.

FELDON GOES INTO HIS PRIVATE OFFICE WHILE BONNIE
RETURNS TO STUDYING THE FILE.

                                        FADE OUT.

Chapter 11

The Night is Always Dark

(This screenplay was completed in 1993 but was based on a radio play entitled "He Who Laughs Last" from 1989. A spoof of film noir written in the 'crowbar in as many jokes as possible style, the script was optioned after being posted on the Trigger Street website in 2008. Sadly the film was never produced. The option, however, did spur me to get back to writing new screenplays.)

FADE IN:

EXT. LOS ANGELES - NIGHT

Familiar Los Angeles sites: Sunset Boulevard, The Hollywood sign, downtown area.

> MAN (V.O.)
> Los Angeles. City of the Angels. Angels
> of Dread, Deceit, and Despair. A dirty
> city with a million dirty secrets, and I
> know every one of them. Unfortunately.
> Thank God I don't live there.

EXT. BIG CITY - NIGHT

Downtown Big City, a fictional metropolis. Neon lights flash. Shadowy people walk through the urban jungle. Steam rises from a gutter as a taxi passes by.

> MAN (V.O.) CONT'D
> I live here. Big City. All that information
> isn't much use to me here. Big City. A
> million strangers trying to scratch and
> claw their way to the top of the heap. A
> few make it. Most end up back where
> they started, figuring out the odds on
> their next long shot. These are my streets.
> This is my city. Did I mention I live
> here?

INT. FEAR'S OFFICE – NIGHT

HARRISON FEAR (40), world weary, reasonably good looking, is calm but intense. He wears brown slacks and a loosened tie over a rumpled dress-shirt.

He stands at the window of his office, contemplating the passing parade of life on the street below.

An ancient Royal typewriter sits on his desk amidst a mess of papers. An open filing cabinet with a few liquor bottles and glasses on it. A threadbare couch covered by a faded trenchcoat.

> FEAR (V.O.)
> The name's Harrison Fear. I'm a P.I. I'd
> been up half the night and awake the
> other half. I felt like a stranger in Big
> City.

Fear bends to the window to peer more closely at the street below.

> FEAR (V.O.)
> I felt so totally alone, completely
> removed from all those people down on
> the street below. From up here they
> looked like ants.
> (looks closer)
> Wait a minute, those are ants.

Fear wipes the window. He winces, flicks an ant off the pane. He sits
behind his desk.

> FEAR (V.O.) CONT'D
> You probably know the feeling. It's like a
> bottle of cheap champagne. You know
> the cork is bound to blow off, but you
> know if it does it'll get your fingers all
> sticky and messy. But down these sticky
> and messy streets a man must walk. As
> long as he doesn't have his good shoes
> on.

A KNOCK on the door.

> FEAR
> It's open.

SGT. DANIEL HYGIENE of the Big City Police Department enters.
Fiftyish, heavy-set, and chomping a cigar, he wears a suit badly in
need of a press.

> FEAR
> Well, if it isn't my old partner, Sergeant
> Hygiene. That a cigar in your mouth or
> you just glad to see me?

                    HYGIENE
        Hello, Harry. Still peeping through
        keyholes in cheap motels?

                    FEAR
        Yeah. I'm also a private
        detective. It's been a while. Social call?

                    HYGIENE
        Business.

                    FEAR
        Pull up a chair.

Hygiene picks up a chair and takes it to the front of the desk, but
continues to stand.

                    FEAR
        You can sit in it.

Hygiene puts down the chair and sits in it.

                    HYGIENE
        It's being reopened, Harry.

                    FEAR
        What's being reopened?

                    HYGIENE
        Don't play dumb. The Zalluza case.
        There's a new D.A. in office and he
        doesn't like loose threads.

                    FEAR
        Then tell him to get a new tailor.

                    HYGIENE
        Don't be such a wiseguy, Fear. It's time
        to wake up and smell the music.

                    FEAR
        Well, you know I always support my
        local police.

                    HYGIENE
You used to be a cop yourself, Harry. A
man of respect. What happened to you?

                    FEAR
I dunno. I became an ex-cop. That's
respectable.

Hygiene walks over to the couch and flops down. Fear gets up and
sits in Hygiene's chair.

                    HYGIENE
Nah, you're just a down and out private
dick with plenty of ulcers and twice as
many unpaid bills.

Fear looks contemplative.

                    FEAR
Tell me about it.

                    HYGIENE
Most of them are from your ulcer
specialist. You're in hock from the tippy-
top of your three-dollar haircut to the
bippity-bottom of your rented underwear.
You call a cheap two room walk-up
home, even though you live at the
downtown Howard Johnson's.

                    FEAR
You know me, Serge. All I need is a
place to hang my hat. And a hat.

Hygiene jumps to his feet.

                    HYGIENE
Well, I just thought I'd tell you about the
Zalluza case.

Fear jumps to his feet.

                    FEAR
Figure you owe me something?

                    HYGIENE
          That was the past, Harry. It was my job.
          I'm sorr...

Fear moves closer to him.

                    FEAR
          Forget about the past. I've tried to forget
          about the past every day of my life.

                    HYGIENE
          If you were me you would have done the
          same thing in my place.

Hygiene moves closer to Fear.

                    FEAR
          Put yourself in my place. A man in my
          position would never be in your shoes.

                    HYGIENE
          If you were in my shoes you would have
          done the same thing I did in your place.

Fear gets in his face.

                    FEAR
          Get out of my place. And wipe my shoes
          you're in.

                    HYGIENE
          You want me to leave?

                    FEAR
          Yeah, you know how to leave don't you?
          Go to the door...

Hygiene goes to the door.

                    FEAR
          Take your hand...

Hygiene raises his left hand.

                    FEAR
              No, your other hand.

Hygiene raises his right hand.

                    FEAR
              Put it around the knob.

Hygiene grabs the doorknob.

                    FEAR
              Open the door.

Hygiene opens the door.

                    FEAR
              Lift your left leg.

Hygiene lifts his left leg.

                    FEAR
              Stick out your tongue.

Hygiene sticks out his tongue.

                    FEAR
              Cross your eyes, and leave.

Hygiene crosses his eyes.

                    FEAR
              See ya later.

                  HYGIENE
              Zee ya ladul.

Hygiene hops out of the office and closes the door. Fear walks to his desk.

                    FEAR (V.O.)
          Yeah, I knew I'd be seeing my old pal
          Sergeant Hygiene because... I see him all
          the time. But that didn't worry me. I
          knew that behind that rough exterior he
          had a heart of gold. I also knew that
          behind the underwear in his sock drawer
          he had a lot of muscleman magazines.
          Sure, Hygiene was nothing to write home
          about. But he could call once in a while.
          After all, it wouldn't kill him, the rates on
          the weekend are sixty percent lower.

The telephone on Fear's desk RINGS. He picks it up.

                    FEAR
          Fear here.

INT. LIZ'S HOUSE - NIGHT INTERCUT WITH FEAR

LIZ TYLER (35) is an elegantly dressed, breathtaking blonde. She's
the kind of woman who's been around just enough to get where she
is.

                    LIZ
          Hello, Harry.

Fear's jaw drops.

                    LIZ
          Harry?

                    FEAR
          Yeah. Hello.

                    LIZ
          This is—

                    FEAR
          I know who it is. Hello, Liz.
                    LIZ
          Been a long time.

FEAR
Ten years. Ten long, lonely years. One
decade. Of loneliness. One long, lonely--

LIZ
I hadn't realized.

FEAR
I had.
LIZ
That was a long time ago, Harry.

FEAR
Yeah, ten years ago, ten long—

LIZ
Yeah, ten years ago, right.

FEAR
So, you calling about something or just
practicing the theme from "The
Jefferson"'" on your touch-tone?

LIZ
Oh, don't be silly Harry. You know I lost
the sheet music to that years ago. I need
to see you.

FEAR
Need to see me, huh?

LIZ
Yes. Could you come over at about nine?

FEAR
Sure, why not?

LIZ
Well, looking forward to seeing you
then.

FEAR
That's generally the best direction to
face.

END INTERCUT

Fear hangs up the phone.

> FEAR (V.O.)
> I hung up on her.

He relaxes and looks away from the phone, then quickly looks back, grabs it and quickly dials.

> FEAR (V.O.)
> Then I called her back to find out what
> the hell her address was.

LATER

Fear puts on his trenchcoat and dark brown snap-brim fedora. He takes a gun out of his desk and puts it in his trenchcoat.

> FEAR (V.O.)
> It was a hot night, hot enough to smoke
> meat and be thankful for the privilege. I
> was in a hurry. Sure, I'd been running
> away from my past. But now I was trying
> to catch up with my future, and boy were
> my legs tired. After all, it had been ten
> years since I'd seen her face, her
> beautiful face I swore I'd never see again.
> She was the kind of dame you like to
> keep at your fingertips, but at arm's
> length.

Fear pulls the brim of his hat down.

> FEAR (V.O,)
> Sure, she was no angel, but who was I?
> An ex-Marine who left the police force
> under a cloud of suspicion to work as a
> freelance investigative consultant.

Fear walks to the door and opens it. He adjusts his coat. On the door's glass pane are the words:

"Harrison fear, an ex-Marine who left the police force under a cloud of suspicion to work as a Freelance Investigative Consultant."

Fear walks into the corridor and closes the door.

I/E. FEAR'S CAR - NIGHT

Fear drives an old sports car badly in need of a paint job. Drops of rain. Fear turns on his wipers.

> FEAR (V.O.)
> Ten years. Ten long, lone-- Ah, screw
> it. It was ten years ago. Get over it.

Fear is lost in his thoughts as the rain falls harder.

> FEAR (V.O.)
> Ten years is a long time. I
> wondered if Liz had changed, or if she
> just acted differently.

Fear shakes his head and laughs.

> FEAR (V.O.)
> Who was I kidding? People don't change.
> I didn't think that ten years ago but I do
> now. People keep doing the same things,
> telling the same lies, pulling the same
> boners. If I had a quarter for every time
> some joker made a mistake he'd made
> before I'd be playing Ms. PacMan for the
> next twenty years.

EXT. LIZ'S MANSION - NIGHT

Fear drives into an elegant estate and parks in front of an imposing mansion.

Fear gets out of the car and fight through the rain to the front stoop. He removes his hat and knocks on the front door.

Out of curiosity, he quickly checks the mailbox.

Liz opens the door.

> LIZ
> Hello, Harry.

> FEAR
> Been a long time.

> LIZ
> Yes, you said that.

Fear and Liz enter the house. THUNDER ROARS.

INT. LIZ'S HOUSE – NIGHT

Liz and Fear walk through the foyer to a fashionably decorated sitting room.

> LIZ
> How've you been Harry?

> FEAR
> How I've been Harry I'll never know, but
> somehow I've managed.

Fear looks her over.

Fear sits.

> FEAR
> You've never looked more lovely. But
> then, neither have I.

> LIZ
> Please, have a chair.

> FEAR
> No thanks, I already have one.

> LIZ
> No, not seat, chair.

                    FEAR
          Oh, sorry. I had my mind on... other
          things.

                    LIZ
          Would you like a whiskey?

                    FEAR
          I certainly would.

                    LIZ
          Well, next time you have one I'm sure
          you'll enjoy it.

Fear suddenly leans forward.

                    FEAR
          How is...?
                    LIZ
          Oh, he's fine.

                    FEAR
          When is...?

                    LIZ
          He'll be back in a few hours.

                    FEAR
          Where is...?

                    LIZ
          He's at his club.

                    FEAR
          Now, where's the bathroom? I
          thought I might freshen up a...

                    LIZ
          Harry, I gave the servants the night off
          because...

Liz moves her lips but there is no sound. Fear is slightly more
attentive, worrying he may have missed something.

                    FEAR
          What was that?

                    LIZ
          Don't worry, it had nothing to do with the
          plot. Harry, I brought
          you here for a reason.

Fear leans back and relaxes.

                    FEAR
          You do everything for a reason.

Liz squeezes into the chair with Fear.

                    LIZ
          Harry, you can't know, you can't imagine
          what I've been through these past ten
          long, lonely...

The chair is too small for both of them and Fear squirms.

                    FEAR
          I can take a guess. My heart bleeds for
          you.

                    LIZ
          I suppose we all have our crosses to bear.

                    FEAR
          Yeah, only you can hire people to carry
          yours. I got nailed to mine.

                    LIZ
          That's the past, Harry. Those days are
          over.

                    FEAR
          For you, maybe.

Liz squirms in the chair.

                    LIZ
          Please, Harry. I need your help. I
          understand you're a private investigator.

> FEAR
> It's not a difficult concept to grasp. And
> that's P.I. to you.

> LIZ
> I have a job for you. An
> assignment.

Fear squeezes out of the chair and stands.

> FEAR
> Well, which is it and how much does it
> pay? I charge two hundred a day plus
> expenses. For starters.

> LIZ
> How much do you charge without the
> starters?

> FEAR
> One seventy-five, but that's as low as I
> go.

> LIZ
> What would you say to five thousand?

> FEAR
> I'd say it was the square root of twenty-
> five million. What's the job?

> LIZ
> I must warn you, Harry. It may be
> dangerous.

> FEAR
> Danger is my middle name. It used to be
> Eugene but I changed it for professional
> reasons. Danger's part of the job. In order
> to be a P.I. you've got to be part
> detective, a little mind reader, a bit
> researcher, a quarter bodyguard, a
> smidgeon chauffeur, nineteen point two
> six percent receptionist, mostly cynic and
> all skeptic.

                    LIZ
          You weren't always like this, Harry. Do
          you remember?

                    FEAR
          Yeah, I remember. I remember all too
          well.

INT. POLICE STATION - FLASHBACK (1979) - DAY

SUSPECTS, uniformed PATROLMEN and plain clothes
DETECTIVES are in the Detective Squad room. Fear and Hygiene
are hard at work behind their desks.

                    FEAR (V.O.)
          I think it was ten years ago, wasn't it? Or
          maybe it was twenty three and a half.
          The place was the squad room of
          Precinct Forty- Two. My partner was
          Daniel Hygiene. I called him Dan. We
          called ourselves detectives, even though
          we actually worked for the fire
          department. Something about our
          applications getting mixed up downtown,
          I don't know...

                                        DISSOLVE TO:

INT. POLICE STATION - FLASHBACK (1979) - DAY

Same as previous scene. Fear and Hygiene work at different desks.

                    FEAR (V.O.)
          After about a week we finally got things
          straightened out. We were detectives in
          the Big City Police Department. Only
          now for some reason we called ourselves
          firemen.

Hygiene types a report.

                    FEAR
          Did you wrap up that Connelly
          homicide?

> HYGIENE
> Yeah, finally, but it was no duckwalk,
> Harry. Wilson didn't make a single
> mistake, except for leaving the body and
> the murder weapon in his living room.
> But it was his confession that nailed him.

> FEAR
> Yeah, his confession was the icing on the
> cake.

A cake lies on a tray near their desks. Icing on the cake reads:

"I DID IT. WILSON."

Hygiene finishes the report.

> HYGIENE
> Baker, take this to records.

BAKER, dressed in a chef's hat and apron, wheels the cake tray out.

> FEAR
> Now maybe you can give me some help
> on that Zalluza case. He's a tough nut to
> crack.

> HYGIENE
> Yeah, I've had tough nuts in my time.

OFFICER LATRINE, an enthusiastic young patrolman, comes over
to their desks. He speaks to Hygiene.

> LATRINE
> Excuse me, have you seen Lieutenant
> Von Bulow, Sergeant?

> HYGIENE
> Yeah, he's over there giving Danzano the
> third degree.

Across the room is LT. VON BULOW, a by-the-book, no-nonsense policeman dressed in a suit with his coat off, sleeves rolled up and badge on his belt.

He shakes hands with DANZANO, a grinning idiot in a graduation gown and mortarboard, and hands him a diploma.

Etched on the squad room door next to them: "Robbery, Homicide and unauthorized Nipsey Russell Impersonations".

ROOSTER LEE JACKSON walks in, dressed in a suede jacket, gold chains, and wide-brimmed hat with a white feather.

> FEAR (V.O.)
> Rooster Lee Jackson showed up, looking
> the way he always does when we call
> him downtown - like a cheap, two-bit
> thug, even though he works for the fire
> department too.

Jackson smiles as he is greeted by TWO UNIFORMED FIREMEN who escort him out.

An OFFICER escorts JOE ZALLUZA, a gangster whose custom-tailored suit can't hide his cheap arrogance.

> FEAR
> Well, well. Look what the playful but
> deadly tiger cub dragged in. Joe Zalluza,
> as I live and retch.

> ZALLUZA
> You better have a good reason for
> hauling me in, Fear. I have a very
> expensive lawyer, and he's half Jewish.

> FEAR
> Oh, yeah? Which half?

> ZALLUZA
> The half that knows how to diversify my
> portfolio and-- wait a minute. It's the
> other half.

(MORE)

                    ZALLUZA (cont'd)
          The half that bites. One slip and I'll have
          your job.

Fear stands abruptly and his chair crashes behind him, hitting a
POLICEMAN who is bent down tying his shoe. The shoes are
oversized clown shoes and he does a comedic tumble.

                    FEAR
          You can have my job, as long as I get
          you behind bars. Your days are
          numbered.

                    ZALLUZA
          No they're not. They're named. Monday,
          Tuesday, Wednesday--

                    FEAR
          A tough guy, huh? I knew a tough guy
          once. Now he's six feet under.

                    ZALLUZA
          Six feet under where?

                    FEAR
          No, thirty-eight large.

                    HYGIENE
          We can do without the banter, Zalluza.
          Or maybe your wife or girlfriend or
          concubine or Little Bo Peep can't. But
          for now, we'd like to ask you a few
          questions.

                    FEAR
               (contemptuously)
          Or maybe you'd like to wait for your...
          lawyer. I guess without him you feel a
          little naked, punk.

                    ZALLUZA
          I haven't felt like a little naked punk in
          years.

Zalluza and Fear sit.

> HYGIENE
> Where were you on the night of July
> eighteenth?

> ZALLUZA
> 3072 Halsted Street, Chicago, watching
> my aunt open for Kool and the Gang.

> FEAR
> Who killed Ritchie the Rat?

> ZALLUZA
> Oh, something happen to Ritchie?

> HYGIENE
> We found his body in your breakfast
> nook.

> ZALLUZA
> Cops. Find a body and right away you
> think somebody's been killed.

> FEAR
> That won't wash, Zalluza. Come clean.

> ZALLUZA
> I've been through the wringer before. No
> soap.

Fear stands up and confronts him.

> FEAR
> You think you're pretty smart, don't you?
> Well, tell me how many dimples in a golf
> ball. You're too smart for your own good,
> Mr. Dehumidifier Repair School
> Dropout. Someday I'm going to bring
> you down to police headquarters and grill
> you until you beg for mercy.

> HYGIENE
> Uh, Harry, that's today.

                    FEAR
          You think I can't touch you. You have
          your alibis, your witnesses, you may
          even be innocent, but none of that
          matters. The only thing that matters is
          that you end up like your kind always
          does, and if our overcrowded judicial
          system can't take care of you then I will,
          personally.

Zalluza stands and walks closer to Fear.

                  ZALLUZA
          You can't talk to me that way. I run this
          town. This is my city.

                    FEAR
          Are you crazy? This is my city.

                  ZALLUZA
          In your hat. This is my city. And it's my
          turf.

Fear moves closer to Zalluza.

                    FEAR
          Well, they're my streets.

                  ZALLUZA
          No way. The South Side's in my back
          pocket, the lakefront's in my coat, and
          the dock's in my vest.

                  HYGIENE
          You must have quite an ironing bill.

                  ZALLUZA
          Around here I'm my own boss.

Fear gets into Zalluza's face.

                    FEAR
          Yeah, but are you your own man?

> ZALLUZA
> I don't have to be. I'm my own best
> friend.

> FEAR
> And your own worst enemy. And your
> nose hair needs trimming.

> ZALLUZA
> Maybe so. The five of us are leaving.
> And for your information, I don't trim it.
> I'm cultivating it.

Zalluza backs away from Fear.

> ZALLUZA
> What's the point talking to you guys?
> This whole thing's a raw deal.

> FEAR
> Or maybe you're just drawing to an
> inside straight?

> ZALLUZA
> Nah, I think the deck is stacked against
> me.

> HYGIENE
> Well, I guess we've reached a stalemate.

Fear leans into Hygiene.

> FEAR
> It's a poker reference, you idiot.

> ZALLUZA
> Oh yeah? Well, pawn to Queen's rook
> three.

Hygiene ponders a moment, then nods in understanding.

> FEAR
> You know, it's guys like you that give
> Italians a bad name.

> ZALLUZA
> I'm not Italian, I'm Armenian.

> FEAR
> I know. Armenians are always insulting
> Italians.

Fear grabs Zalluza by the lapels.

> FEAR
> You make me sick! You won't always
> have your gang around to protect you.
> One of these days when you're alone, I'll
> be there.

> MAN (O.S.)
> Remove your hands from my client.

Fear's head turns. His face reveals the shock of recognition.

MARTIN EDGEMONT walks up. Distinguished, he exudes an aura of subdued intensity.

Fear releases Zalluza.

> EDGEMONT
> I hope you are prepared to answer
> charges of police brutality.

Zalluza straightens his coat and smiles.

> ZALLUZA
> I'd like you to meet my attorney, Martin
> Edg—

> FEAR
> We've met. We're from the same
> neighborhood. Ironic, ain't it? I grew up
> to be an honest cop and you wound up a
> shyster for the mob.

                    EDGEMONT
You're just the sort of uncultured, half-
witted flatfoot I'd expect to resort to the
gutter tactic of name calling.

Edgemont goes to desk. The policeman in clown shoes is sprawled
on the floor.

                    ZALLUZA
You took your sweet time getting here.

                    EDGEMONT
Sorry. The tractor pull was in town, and I
wanted to be sure I'd miss it. I should
have you out of here in a matter of
minutes.

                    FEAR
You must be mighty proud of yourself,
Mr.I-went-to-an-Ivy League-College-
and-got-into-Law-School-through-
connections-so-I- could-represent-
Scumballs-and- Sleazebags-for-money.

                    EDGEMONT
That used to be my name. I changed it to
Edgemont for professional reasons.

                    FEAR (to Zalluza)
You're guilty and everybody knows it.
        (to Hygiene)
Am I right or am I right?

                    HYGIENE
What were the choices again?

Two gruff-looking men, SMOOT and GARRET, slide up.

                    SMOOT
The name's Garrett, Frank Garrett.
        (points to Garrett)
Uh, that's his name. My name's Irwin
Smoot. You probably don't remember me
because we've never met. We're here
from the D.A.'s office. We have a writ

saying that any charges against Zalluza
are to be dropped.

He takes out a piece of paper from his pocket and plants it
authoritatively on the desk.

>   SMOOT
>   That's not it, but if you need some
>   coupons for aluminum siding...

>   GARRETT
>   Zalluza couldn't have committed the
>   murder. The coroner put the time of
>   death between one and three A.M.,
>   giving Zalluza a perfect alibi since he
>   was with me at my
>   place.
>   FEAR
>   Have you thought about what'll happen
>   when you put this thug back on the
>   streets?

>   GARRETT
>   I'll cross that bridge when I come to it.

>   FEAR
>   What if the bridge is up and a large ocean
>   liner is passing, pushed by tugboats and
>   Little
>   Orphan Annie paddling a-

>   GARRETT
>   Okay. I'll rethink that.

Smoot elbows Garrett.

>   SMOOT
>   We're not paid to think.

>   FEAR
>   You certainly earn your salary. All right
>   Zalluza, you can go but don't leave this
>   room.

Zalluza is bewildered. He, Edgemont, Smoot, and Garrett leave desk area.

Edgemont and Zalluza hold hands.

> HYGIENE
> That Edgemont's some big time operator, huh?

> FEAR
> Yeah, if you think a big time operator is supposed to get organized crime figures off the hook just so he can pay the mortgage on his Yahtzee museum.

> HYGIENE
> Sounds like you and Edgemont have crossed paths before.

> FEAR
> No, but we have met. I don't want to talk about it. I'd rather keep it inside me, twisting my guts out until it tears me apart.

> HYGIENE
> Well, Harry, don't let it get you down. We'll get 'em next time.

> FEAR
> (introspectively)
> Yeah, I know. You win some, you lose some. Some are suspended on account of darkness.
> (with belligerence)
> Others are called off because of fan interference. I told them not to sell beer at the ballpark. They were only asking for trouble.

Von Bulow comes over to the desk.

> VON BULOW
> Fear! Office!

Von Bulow storms off while Fear and Hygiene look puzzled. Von Bulow returns to the desk somewhat sedated.

> VON BULOW
> Uh, my office?

Fear leaves with Von Bulow and Hygiene returns to desk.

INT. VON BULOW'S OFFICE – DAY

Fear enters. Von Bulow moves behind his desk.

> VON BULOW
> Harry, the complaints I've had about you
> would fill a filing cabinet.

Von Bulow sits. Fear sits, snatches up a bag of potato chips and munches.

A filing cabinet behind him reads: "Complaints about Harrison Fear".

> FEAR
> And who were the complainers? Sleazy
> hoods? Lowlife hustlers? Limpwristed
> sugardaddies? Banana smoking flower
> children?

> VON BULOW
> It doesn't matter, Harry. Everyone says
> you have a chip on your shoulder.

Fear pauses as he eats a chip. Looks at one shoulder, then the other.

> FEAR
> Oh, yeah? Like who?

> VON BULOW
> Harry, I like a dedicated cop, but you've
> gone overboard.

                    FEAR
Maybe you'd like a cop who punches a
clock. A cop who takes half an hour off
for lunch, gets home at six, eats soggy
mashed potatoes and a tough steak, falls
asleep smoking in bed and gets up the
next day wondering why his pajamas
smell. Well, that's not me. That's my evil
twin brother, Garrison Fear.

                    VON BULOW
I'm warning you, Harry. You're playing
Russian roulette with dynamite. Get in
the game, but play by the rules.

                    FEAR
A cop doesn't need rules. A cop only
needs two things, a Thirty- Eight Special
and six bullets.

                    VON BULOW
That's seven things, Harry. Learn to
count. Look, you've got a week's
vacation coming to you. Take three days
off.

Fear leaves in a huff. As he exits, Zalluza pokes his head in the
room.

                    ZALLUZA
Can I leave yet?

INT. BAR - NIGHT

Fear sits down at the bar. Bartender comes over.

                    BARTENDER
How about a drink?

                    FEAR
Sure.
Fear opens his jacket, takes out a shot glass filled with liquor and
gives it to the Bartender. The Bartender gulps it down, slams down
the glass and leaves.

> LIZ (O.S.)
> You got change for a Series E savings
> bond?

Fear raises an eyebrow.

> FEAR (V.O.)
> I recognized that voice. It was my second
> grade teacher, Ms. Perkins My God she
> was—

Fear whirls around. And is taken aback.

> FEAR (V.O.)
> --attractive as hell. And not Ms. Perkins.

Fear sizes up Liz as a SAX PLAYER nearby strikes up a sultry tune.

> FEAR (V.O.)
> I gave her the once-over a couple of
> times.

Fear gets a good look at her, slowly from her feet up to her face. Liz
looks directly in his eyes.

Fear continues to look upward, past her face and over her head. She
stretches on her toes and strains, trying to keep level with his eyes.

> FEAR (V.O.)
> She was a beautiful babe, a dazzling
> dame, a knockout.

Sounds of BOXING ARENA, the BELL, then the CROWD NOISE.

> FEAR (V.O.)
> A middleweight contender with a great
> right uppercut until she kissed the canvas
> in four rounds against the champ at the
> Garden.

Sounds of BOXING ARENA fade out.

                    FEAR (V.O.)
          Just one look at her and I knew I
          wanted to go the distance. But was I
          stepping out of my class? She parted her
          ruby-red lips and said:

                    LIZ
          Buy me a drink?

                    FEAR
          Sure.

Fear motions to Bartender to come over.

                    BARTENDER
          How about a drink?

                    FEAR
          We did that joke already.
                    (to Liz)
          What's your pleasure?

                    LIZ
          I like being tied up and covered
          with toothpaste.

                    FEAR
          I know. But what would you like to
          drink?

                    LIZ
          I'll just have a Cola, thanks.

                    FEAR
                    (to Bartender)
          Vodka and wolverine milk.

Bartender leaves. Fear and Liz wait for each other to speak.

                    FEAR AND LIZ
          So—

Both are embarrassed to have interrupted the other.

                    FEAR AND LIZ
          I didn't mean to—

Both laugh almost shyly under their breath.

                    FEAR AND LIZ
          Were you going to—

They both have a quick think.

                    FEAR AND LIZ (suspiciously)
          Toyboat.

They each chew their lip, thinking. Intrigued.

                    FEAR AND LIZ
          Hawaii, with an average rainfall of
          eighty-six point nine inches per year.
          Four score and seven years ago, kibbles
          and bits, rock and roll, what on god's
          green earth come on baby, let's do the
          twist--

The Bartender slams their drinks down. Points to Fear.

                    BARTENDER
          You go first.

                    FEAR
          Thank you.
                    (to Liz)
          The name's Fear. Harrison Fear.

                    LIZ
          Liz.

                    FEAR
          Just Liz?

                    LIZ
          Just Liz.

Fear raises his glass in a toast. Liz meets his glass with hers. They
drink.

FEAR (V.O.)
Well, one thing led to another, and when
one thing leads to another its easy to
guess what follows.

INT. FEAR'S APARTMENT - NIGHT

The door opens. Fear and Liz enter. Fear closes the door and turns on
the light.

FEAR
Well, this is it.

LIZ
It's very nice.

FEAR
I have a woman who comes in twice a
week. She takes a shower and leaves
mints on my pillow. She doesn't do any
cleaning. She got hold of one of my keys,
I tried changing the locks—

LIZ
I can imagine what you must think of me,
coming to the apartment of a stranger
I've never met before. Are you shocked?

FEAR
Read my lips, Babe. I escaped from an
Iraqi prison camp by knocking out three
machine-gun nests and napalming an
entire peasant village using only my big
toes. I like a woman who knows what
she wants and how to get it.

LIZ
And I like a man who has the know-how
to get what he wants.

FEAR
And I like a woman who wants what she
knows how to get.

                    LIZ
And I like a man who gets to know what
he wants.

                    FEAR
Yeah, I guess a good man is hard to find.

                    LIZ
And a hard man is good to find.

Fear glances down at his pants.

                    LIZ
Tell me something about Harrison Fear.

                    FEAR
I like to fondle yogurt.

                    LIZ
There must be more to tell than that.

                    FEAR
Just the same old story that's been told a
million times before in Big City. I grew
up on the streets of the South Side. My
mother left home before I was born. My
father was a closet alcoholic.

                    LIZ
Oh?

                    FEAR
Yeah. Still is, too.

Fear goes to the closet and opens the door, revealing a SKID ROW
WINO guzzling from a wine bottle in a brown paper bag. Fear closes
the door. Glass breaks.

                    FEAR
Now, you tell me something about Liz.
Just Liz. No, don't tell me.I bet I know
your whole life story You were raised on
an ant farm in Upper Volta—

Liz holds up a palm to stop him.

> LIZ
> No, no. The past doesn't matter. All that
> matters is now, tonight. It's been a long
> time since I've been with a man.

> FEAR
> Me too.

Liz embraces him. He embraces her.

> FEAR
> You're all woman.

> LIZ
> You're-- a lot of man.

> FEAR
> Not all?

> LIZ
> Not yet.

Liz kisses him passionately. Feels something down below and her
eyes bulge.

> LIZ
> There you go. All man.

> FEAR (V.O.)
> She deserved an Oscar for that
> performance. Or at least a People's
> Choice Award.

INT. DINER – DAY

The classic American greasy spoon. Fear and Hygiene sit at the
counter. A WAITRESS comes over.

> WAITRESS
> What'll you boys have?

FEAR
Well, how about something to eat?

HYGIENE
Not for me, thanks. I'll just have some
lunch.

Waitress writes, then leaves.

HYGIENE
Haven't seen you in a while, partner. The
little woman's been asking about you.
Come on over for dinner sometime.
Don't be a stranger, Jim--

FEAR
(under his breath)
Harry.

HYGIENE
Drop in Sunday night, the missus will
make us some pot roast, maybe some
cherry pie with pistachios.

Waitress brings food.

WAITRESS
We were out of lunch, so I made you
some dinner instead.

Fear and Hygiene tuck napkins in their shirts and roll up their
sleeves. They eat.

HYGIENE
How'd you enjoy your time off?

FEAR
Had its moments.

HYGIENE
Something happen?

FEAR
Could say that

            HYGIENE
You trying not to tell me
something?

            FEAR
No. But I'd rather not talk about it.

            HYGIENE
Whatever you say, partner. You don't
have to hit me over the head with a
sledge hammer. I leave that to others. It's
not something I said? Something I didn't
say? Something I did, something I didn't
do? Something I said I didn't do?
Something I said I'd do but didn't?
Something I didn't say I'd do but did,
something I didn't say I'd say but said I'd
do, something I—

            FEAR
No, it's something, but it's
nothing like that.

            HYGIENE
Is it because your father's a
closet alcoholic?

            FEAR
No, Robert. You wouldn't
understand, you couldn't
understand.

            HYGIENE
I don't understand. And my name's Dan.

            FEAR
 Case in point.

            HYGIENE
If it's the Zalluza case that's bothering
you, don't let it. We're gonna get him.

            FEAR
Of course we will. And Edgemont will
get him off. I mean—spring him, gain
him freedom. Though hell, come to think

FEAR (ctd)
of it, maybe he'll get him off, too. But
that's beside the point.

HYGIENE
Word is the department has a key witness
under raps. You may remember the
name: Leo "The Shiv" Rostelli? Works
with a chain saw.

FEAR
Terrific. Now we've got to baby- sit some
two-bit thug who's living it up at the
taxpayer's expense. Believe me, that
Rostelli is asking for what's coming to
him.

HYGIENE
Easy, Harry. He's turning state's
evidence.

FEAR
Evidence, shmevidence. Rats like that
belong in a cage where they can eat food
pellets and run inside little wheels when
you put No-Doz in their water.

HYGIENE
It's not our place, Harry. That's for
twelve men to decide. And if not them, a
jury.

FEAR
Yeah, and have some bleeding-heart
judge throw the case out on legal
grounds. Damned laws.

HYGIENE
Something tells me it's not just this
Zalluza case bugging you,
Harry. Girl trouble?

FEAR
Let's not get personal here,
Hygiene. Next thing you know, I'll be
saying something just to stick you.

                    FEAR (ctd)
Something like your mother's a dried
sack that never loved you, but ever since
she stopped breast feeding you, you've
been clutching at her chest in the vain
pursuit of dignity. Defines every
relationship you've ever had since.

Hygiene turns away, wounded. Reaches into his pocket, he pulls out
a couple of dollars and puts them on the counter.

He rises, and his eyes land on the Waitress's breasts. Moment, then a
a few tears fall. He leaves.

Fear looks after Hygiene regretfully. He pays his bill and pursues
him.

                    WAITRESS
Leaving so soon? He didn't finish his
lunch. Dinner!

Fear exits.

EXT. DINER - DAY

Fear catches up with Hygiene and stops him.

                    FEAR
Sorry, Dan. I'm out of it today. Didn't
mean that at all - I was just talking about
myself.

Hygiene snaps out of it - completely back to normal, no harm done.

                    HYGIENE
Oh.

                    FEAR
Yeah, it's a girl. How did you know?

                    HYGIENE
I can put two and two together. I can't
add them up, but I can put
them together.

                    FEAR
I can't get anything past you, can I?

                    HYGIENE
Harry, I know you like the back of my
head. Personally, I like my
little bald spot. My wife likes my neck
hairs. I've just switched to pomade
recently and--

                    FEAR
It's a woman alright. Her name is Liz.

                    HYGIENE
Only Liz?

                    FEAR
No, Just Liz. I don't know, Dan, you may
think it's kind of corny, but sometimes I
wonder what it'd be like to find that
special girl, the one you'd want to spend
the rest of your life with.

                    HYGIENE
A lot of guys feel that way, Harry. Not
me, of course. I'd never do anything that
sissy.

Hygiene walks away from the diner and Fear follows. As they talk
the diner remains in b.g.

                    FEAR
You know, Dan, it's strange. I never
thought I'd think this way
about a girl.

                    HYGIENE
You've dated a lot of girls, Harry.

                    FEAR
I know, but this one's had her shots.

A TRAIN WHISTLE BLOWS in the distance.

HYGIENE
I never heard you talk this way before.
With you it's always been love 'em and
leave 'em.

FEAR
Or I leave them first and get it out of the
way. Yeah, I guess I've always been sort
of a lone wolf, even when I was a kid on
the South Side. And then everything
changed. I found a friend. Yeah,
someone I could trust. And he taught me
the greatest lesson I ever learned: You
can never trust anybody.

HYGIENE
You don't really believe that, do you
Harry?

FEAR
Trust me on this one. I learned it in the
desert, killing Mujahadeen who weren't
as quick as me on the trigger. Then I
joined the Marines
and got sent to Iraq.

As we gain distance from the diner, we see that it is located in the
middle of railroad tracks.

The TRAIN WHISTLE blows louder.

HYGIENE
I never knew you were in the war.

FEAR
I don't like to talk about it.

HYGIENE
Sure, I can understa--

FEAR
I did my first tour in ninety-two. I
opened for AC/DC, but my notices were
good and I got moved up to second spot

                  FEAR (ctd)
on the bill. Twelve clicks outside Sadr
City I was on a search and destroy when
I saw something I'll never forget, worse
even than the senseless killing and
destruction going on around me. That
day I lost more than my faith in people. I
lost my faith in faith itself. And to this
day, even in my darkest hour, I blindly
cling to that conviction, dammit.

A train bullets down the tracks and smashes the diner to smithereens.
Fear and Hygiene do not notice.

                  HYGIENE
You have to move on, Harry. That's past.
Dead. History.

                  FEAR
Not to me it isn't. To me it was
yesterday. My sundial's broken.

                  HYGIENE
You're living in the past.

                  FEAR
Yeah, I wish it could be like the old days
when I never lived in the past. I think
about those days all the time.

I/E. CAR (MOVING) - NIGHT

Fear stares impassively at the road before him.

                  HYGIENE (V.O.)
You've got to move on, Harry. That's
past... you're living in the past... that's
dead. Past. History... you've got to move
on, Harry... you're living in the past...

                  TELEVANGELIST (V.O.)
This one time offer is available for your
tax-free donation of nineteen ninety-
five...

ROD SERLING (V.O.)
Submitted for your approval...

RICHARD NIXON (V.O.)
You won't have Richard Nixon to kick
around anymore...

NEVILLE CHAMBERLAIN (V.O.)
I hold in my hand a piece of paper...

BUD ABBOTT (V.O.)
I said, nowadays they give ballplayers
funny names...

JOHN LENNON (V.O.)
I wasn't knocking God as a person, or as
a thing, or whatever He is...

JOHN HOUSEMAN (V.O.)
You come here with a mind full of
mush...

The various V.O.'s blend together and produce pure GIBBERISH.
Only one V.O. remains audible above the rest, still comprehensible
as CAMERA MOVES IN for--

EXTREME CLOSEUP - FEAR'S EYES

HYGIENE (V.O.)
You're living in the past. Living in the
past. Living in the past. Living in the
past. Ditto. Repeats. Etc etc. And so on.
Mr. Past-y Past. The Past Man. The Past-
est hand in the West. Past-or Harrison
Fear, Church of the Sacred Past.

MATCH DISSOLVE:

INT. KINDERGARTEN - FLASHBACK (1975) - DAY The eyes of
LITTLE FEAR (6) look to and fro.

The gorgeous, statuesque TEACHER helps a group of CHILDREN
ready themselves for the playground.

> FEAR (V.O.)
> It was the fall of '75. I was six. It was
> near the end of class. One more play
> period and it'd be back home to my
> dysfunctional family. My outfit was
> jeans and a food- stained t-shirt. We
> called ourselves kids. And in some ways,
> I guess that that's exactly what we were.

EXT. SCHOOLYARD - FLASHBACK (1975)- DAY

The Teacher is off in the distance, flirting with a HIGH SCHOOL BOY in the bushes.

FRANKIE QUINTERO (7) stares at Fear.

> FRANKIE
> What kind of stupid name is Fear?

> FEAR
> It's Harry.

> FRANKIE
> What are you a-feared of, Harry?

A group of kids gather around them, goading and laughing.

Fear's eyes widen as he sees them holding chain saws, axes and whiffle ball bats.

Fear has a moment of calm and relaxes. He walks away from the crowd of kids.

> FRANKIE
> Hey! What is this?

> FEAR
> It's a moment of quiet reflection.

The kids relax and mingle, looking at their watches and mumbling.

Fear goes to a nearby tree and sits down. He takes a note out of his jacket and reads it.

> SENSITIVE FEMALE
> VOICE (V.O.)
> Dear Son, I hope you are enjoying the
> extra treat I put in your lunch box.
> Everyday I pray you don't get beaten up
> by those boys in leather jackets, or
> spontaneously combust and burst into
> flames.

The Teacher and the High School Kid laugh and light up cigarettes.

> SENSITIVE FEMALE
> VOICE (V.O.)
> You'll always do what you feel is right.

> FEAR
> Jeez. I'm only six.

Fear's arm bursts into flame. He swats at it, stamps it out. Fear puts the note back in his pocket, stands and confronts

Frankie and the other kids.

> FRANKIE
> Looks like you don't have anyone on
> your side, Fearful.

> FEAR
> I have right on my side.

The kids burst into laughter.

> FEAR
> And besides. There is nothing to fear but
> Fear--

Fear is hit in the face with a wad of dirt. He runs for the Teacher.

> SENSITIVE FEMALE
> VOICE (V.O.)
> If you are hit with a flying object...

Fear jumps over the teeter totter and weaves through the jungle gym as the kids give chase.

He takes out his mother's note.

> SENSITIVE FEMALE
> VOICE (V.O.)
> ... if you are overwhelmed by the odds...

Fear looks around, puzzled where the voice is coming from. The kids catch up to Fear before he can reach the Teacher.

But they all stop, too, looking around for the voice.

> FRANKIE
> Who is that?

> SENSITIVE FEMALE
> VOICE (V.O.)
> ... if the hordes that are after you are
> stymied by an unusual voice... just
> remember you'll be
> home soon, and I'm looking forward to
> seeing you, which is the best direction to
> face, as someone said earlier in the film.

The bullies back off, spooked.

> SENSITIVE FEMALE
> VOICE (V.O.)
> But I won't be there, because of my
> experimental facial reconstruction
> surgery, and you'll have to fix your own
> dinner because I caught your dad
> cheating and he's staying in a hotel, and
> your brother was arrested for dealing and
> will be upstate for many years... but I
> digress. Harry, I hope to see you soon,
> but if you don't recognize me I'll be
> wearing a red dress with a white
> carnation. Love... the woman you know
> as your mother.

COUGHING, then the voice becomes low.

> GRUFF MALE VOICE (V.O.)
> Signed, your father.

Fear puts the note in his pocket, confused.

EDGEMONT (at 6), swings off the jungle gym and lands in front of
Fear.

> FEAR
> Who are you?

> EDGEMONT
> Martin. Martin Edgemont.

Martin pulls out a pack of cigarettes.

> EDGEMONT
> You want one?

> FEAR
> Nah. I'm trying to quit.

> EDGEMONT
> This isn't the time for that. When you get
> back into class, there'll be a gang of
> bloodthirsty kids waiting to rip out your
> guts, hang your face from the ceiling,
> burn your--

> FEAR
> I get the picture. Why help me?

> EDGEMONT
> I don't like the odds.

> FEAR
> But we're outnumbered thirteen to one!

> EDGEMONT
> Hmm. That's one way of looking at it.
> But you know what, I want to grow up to
> be a lawyer, defending scumbags and
> ne'er do wells, fast- buck con artists,
> contemptible goons, and foul-minded
> ruffians, not to mention beautiful young

women with large estates and elderly
husbands.

                    FEAR
What does that have to do with me? I'm
just a kid. And so are you.

                    EDGEMONT
Gotta start somewhere, and you're a
sorry piece of work. You're new around
here, right? Where you from?

                    FEAR
Big City.

                    EDGEMONT
Oh, yeah? Me too. South Side.

                    FEAR
Yeah? Me too. Thirty-seventh and
Alamo.

                    EDGEMONT
Yeah? Me too. Maybe we'll be friends
when we grow up.

                                        DISSOLVE TO::

EXT. BIG CITY - FLASHBACK (1979) - DAY

Brownstone buildings from a typical 30's studio New York street. A
street sign reads: "37th" and "Alamo."

FEAR (at 10), wears his trademark hat and leans against the signpost
with EDGEMONT (at 10), who wears a three-piece suit.

                    FEAR
Remember, back when we grew up? We
were just kids then.

                    EDGEMONT
Well, we were a lot younger in those
days.

> FEAR
> Yeah, we did all the things kids do when they're young: collecting baseball cards...

DISSOLVE TO:

INT. CELLAR CLUBHOUSE - FLASHBACK (1975) - DAY

Fear and Edgemont (at 6) look over baseball cards and compare them, excited.

EXT. BIG CITY STREET - FLASHBACK (1975) DAY

> FEAR (AT 10) (V.O.)
> Playing stickball...

A group of boys play ball. Fear (at 6) pitches a well-worn ball to Edgemont who hits a high fly ball.

The ball crashes through the front window of the Kaufmanm Window Factory.

CRASH after CRASH of breaking glass from inside the factory. Fear and Edgemont cringe at each one.

They exchange a look, slowly edge back, then turn and run for their lives.

DISSOLVE TO:

EXT. BIG CITY PARK - FLASHBACK (1975) – DAY

Leafless trees. A thick layer of snow.

> FEAR (AT 10) (V.O.)
> Building a snowman...

Fear and Edgemont work on a snowman. They come to a rest, step back, and take in their work with satisfaction.

The snowman is a replica of Michelangelo's David, save for the missing nose. With great care, Fear takes a carrot out of his coat and places it.

The boys smile at one another, proud.

DISSOLVE TO:

INT. TREEHOUSE - FLASHBACK (1975) - DAY

The boys sit on the floor face to face, cross-legged.

> FEAR (AT 10) (V.O.)
> We performed the ancient ceremony of
> becoming blood brothers.

Edgemont cuts Fear's finger with a pen knife.

> FEAR (AT 6)
> Motherf-- AHEM!!!!!!

Fear stares hard at Edgemont as he takes the knife. He leans forward to cut Edgemont's finger.

> FEAR (AT 10) (V.O.)
> Unfortunately, I got a little overzealous,
> and we forgot you were a hemophiliac.

EXT. TREEHOUSE - FLASHBACK (1975) - DAY

Marty drops out of the treehouse and runs across the yard. His hand squirts blood like a firehouse.

He collapses in mid-run, lies unconscious no the ground. Fear hops down from the treehouse.

> FEAR (AT 6)
> Help!

A MEDIC lies nearby in a hammock, taking in the sun and reading a paper.

He glances up, sees Edgemont, and hustles to his feet.

                                                    DISSOLVE TO:

EXT. BIG CITY - FLASHBACK (1979) - DAY Fear and Edgemont
play in the street.

                    FEAR (AT 10) (V.O.)
            We even played cops and robbers.

                    FEAR (AT 6)
            I wanna be a cop, so I can get all the fast-
            buck con artists, contemptible goons, and
            foul-minded ruffians off the streets.

                    EDGEMONT (AT 6)
            I don't want to be the robber, that's
            unethical. I want to be the defense
            attorney who gets the robber off due to
            our misguided legal system. And it goes
            without saying that I would like to get
            into male modeling, as well.

                                                    DISSOLVE TO:

EXT. BIG CITY - FLASHBACK (1979) - DAY

From their signpost at 37th and Alamo, the boys study a nearby fruit
stand, owned and operated by an excitable European PROPRIETOR.

                    FEAR (AT 10) (V.O.)
            But when it came to robbery for realsies,
            you no longer had any qualms.

                    EDGEMONT (AT 6)
            Okay, when he goes in we'll take some
            fruit from his stand. And be sure to get
            some qualms.

> FEAR (AT 6)
> I can't go along with this.

> EDGEMONT (AT 6)
> What do you mean, you can't go along
> with it?

> FEAR (AT 6)
> I have a code. Maybe it's a crazy kind of
> code, but I have it, and it's mine. We need
> rules.

Edgemont walks toward the fruit stand.

> EDGEMONT (AT 6)
> Rules are made to be broken.

Edgemont moves to the fruit stand. When the Proprietor's back is turned, Edgemont grabs some fruit. He runs away, but catches his foot on a leg of the stand.

The stand tumbles to the ground and fruit scatters everywhere.

Edgemont scrambles to his feet and runs. He stuffs an orange in Fear's front shirt pocket as he races by, then disappears around the corner.

The Proprietor gets to his feet and sees Fear. Red with anger, he snatches Fear by the arm.

DISSOLVE TO:

EXT. SCHOOLYARD - FLASHBACK (1975) - DAY

The dissolve has left a watery blur on the camera.

Barely visible, Fear and Edgemont sit on the teeter totter.

> FEAR (AT 6)
> Yeah, we'll probably be friends, trusting
> each other, relying on each other to look
> out for--

Fear stops talking and looks at the camera. He takes a cloth from his pocket and wipes the mist from the lens.

> FEAR (AT 6)
> To look out for each other. Heck, you'll probably even take a rap for me at some point.

The Bullies have reconvened in a big way - now there's twice as many. Sporting camouflage and combat gear, they signal to one another as the maneuver through the playground towards Fear and Edgemont.

Edgemont's eyes bulge.

> EDGEMONT (AT 6)
> Harry, distract them while I run for safety!

Edgemont jumps off the teeter totter, and Fear crashes down hard, topples into the sand.

He looks up, horrified, as the commando bullies surround him.

EXTREME CLOSEUP - FEAR'S EYES

MATCH DISSOLVE:

INT. FEAR'S APARTMENT - NIGHT

CAMERA PULLS BACK from Fear's eyes to reveal Liz sitting beside him on sofa.

> FEAR
> He got away and I spent a year in the brig. Then we grew up. While Marty Edgemont lived in his ivory tower, I got a one-way ticket to Palookaville. Of course, he did score me a reservation at the Palookaville Hilton. Yeah, every minute of every hour of every one of those days I swore I'd never trust anyone again. Look out for number one. Every man for himself. Kick a man until he's down and

then keep kicking until he can't get up
again.

          LIZ
Harry!
    (holds his hand)
It's alright, Harry. You're just having
childhood flashbacks.

         FEAR
I'm sorry. It's just that whenever I think
about those days something just... But
those days are over now. They're in the
past. I guess I've changed.

Some STRANGE GUY opens the front door and looks at them.

He leaves.

       STRANGE GUY
Harry, my you've changed! You used to
be sullen and morose, but now you seem
much happier. Maybe we could grab a
drink and-- Whoa, wait a second. Wrong
room.

         LIZ
I guess I don't care what happened in the
past. The past doesn't matter. The only
thing that matters now is us. Together.
From now on it's you and me straight
down the line.

         FEAR
Tonight I told you things I thought I'd
never tell anyone, much less another
person.

         LIZ
Harry, you can tell me anything.

         FEAR
Even... I love you?

                    LIZ
        Even that.

They kiss.

He circles around to reveal that Liz is standing in the water, waist high. Fear rows away and gives her a friendly wave. Liz waves back and wades to shore.

EXT. PARK - DAY

Fear, in fedora and trenchcoat, and Liz, in an elegant dress, walk through the park, arm-in-arm and laughing. Until they pass--

Their DOUBLES. The four look each other over in confusion. Fear and his Double exchange puzzled glances upward, fixing on the other's hat. Fear takes his hat off and motions for the Double to remove his.

The Double does so and the two trade hats. Both are satisfied with the fit.

The two couples go their separate ways.

CAMERA FOLLOWS the Doubles as they walk off. After a few steps the Doubles realize. They shoo the camera in the direction of Fear and Liz.

CAMERA PANS QUICKLY to Fear and Liz walking off.

EXT. BIG CITY STREET – DAY

Fear and Liz walk down the street hand in hand. A freshly tossed pizza crust hits Fear on the head, covers his face. Liz looks up tentatively.

EXT. HILLTOP - NIGHT

Fear and Liz gaze wide-eyed at the stars. Fear points out a particular star to Liz. She can't make it out. He points again. She squints, but still can't see it.

Annoyed, Fear pulls a telescope out of his pocket and shoves it into her hands.

She looks through the telescope and nods.

INT. FEAR'S APARTMENT - DAY

Fear sits at the table in his bathrobe, reads a newspaper. Liz enters, wearing Fear's shirt. She sits across from him and they gaze romantically into each other's eyes.

Reveal a MIDGET in front of Fear, holding the paper for him. The Midget folds up the paper, puts it on the table, and leaves without ceremony.

INT. DRESS SHOP - DAY

A parade of models show dresses to Fear and Liz. Liz likes all of them, but Fear registers his dissatisfaction with each.

A model shows a dress and Liz waits for Fear's opinion. He smiles and shakes his head "yes."

EXT. DRESS SHOP - DAY

Fear and Liz come out. Fear wears the dress.

INT. FEAR'S APARTMENT – NIGHT

Fear and Liz prepare dinner. They do not notice a cat entering the kitchen.

The cat hops into the open microwave. Fear doesn't notice, puts a plate of food in and closes the door. Turns the microwave on.

Fear and Liz prepare drinks.

Fear opens microwave and pulls out plate with cat skeleton on it. Liz is horrified. Fear looks at microwave, not knowing what else might come out, then looks back at cat's remains.

EXT. AMUSEMENT PARK - DAY

Fear tries to knock down milk bottles with a baseball. He throws one baseball after another, but no luck.

He throws softballs - nothing.

He throws basketballs - nothing.

He pulls out his gun and fires furiously at the bottles - nothing.

Fear aims his gun at the terrified BARKER. The Barker gives him a giant teddy bear.

EXT. BEACH - NIGHT

Fear and Liz hold hands on a romantic moonlit stroll. Fear gazes longingly at Liz.

> FEAR
> Wait! Stop right where you are. You look
> so perfect, I just want to stand here and
> look at you in this light.

> LIZ (pleased)
> Harry.

Fear moves out of frame. Liz follows his instructions.

> FEAR (O.S.)
> Just, just move your head to the right a
> little bit... now throw back your hair...
> that's fine, now move over to the left a
> little... great... now lift your right
> shoulder... look over this way. Try this on.

Fear's hand comes into frame and he gives her a tube of lipstick. She applies it.

> FEAR (O.S.)
> Here's a stole.

He hands her a stole. She fumbles into the outfit.

DISSOLVE TO:

EXT. FEAR'S BALCONY - NIGHT

Fear and Liz embrace, take in the Big City lights.

> LIZ
> Oh, Harry. Last night seems like only
> yesterday. We've had such a good time
> together.

> FEAR
> You look more beautiful standing here
> than you do sitting down.

> LIZ (touched)
> Harry. This is such a beautiful spot. I
> could spend the rest of my life here if I
> didn't leave.

> FEAR
> See that lot over there? One day I'd like to
> build a little honeymoon cottage. You can
> live there, too.

INT. FEAR'S APARTMENT - NIGHT

They enter.

> FEAR
> It's funny. Used to be the only thing I
> believed in was being a cop. And now?

> LIZ
> Now I believe in two things.

They kiss as the lights go off and plunge the room into darkness.

> LIZ (startled)
> Harry.

              FEAR
Nothing to worry about. Just a power
outage. Happens all the
time.

              LIZ
But I'm afraid of the dark.

The lights come back on.

              FEAR
See? There's nothing to be afraid of in the
dark.
            (sinisterly)
Unless there's somebody in it with a knife
trying to kill you!

              LIZ
Harry!

              FEAR
I'm only teasing.

The lights go off again. The BANG! of a pistol.

The lights come on again. Harry holds a smoking gun in the direction
of a masked ATTACKER, dead on the floor with a knife.

Fear embraces Liz. They kiss.

              FEAR
You've got nothing to be afraid of in the
dark. That is, as long as I'm around.

Fear turns down the dimmer.

INT. FEAR'S APARTMENT - NIGHT

A roaring fireplace.

            LIZ (O.S.)
This is so romantic.

                    FEAR (O.S.)
          I hoped you'd like it.

                    LIZ (O.S.)
          It's very nice.

Fear and Liz sweat profusely on sofa.

                    LIZ
          But could you put it out? It's the middle of
          July and a hundred and five in here.

Liz wipes her brow as Fear stokes out the fire.

                    FEAR
          I just wanted tonight to be
          special.

                    LIZ
          Yes. We've said a lot of things tonight,
          Harry.

                    FEAR
          Some of them even in English.

He puts out the fire and joins Liz on the sofa.

                    FEAR
          I've got something for you.

          He takes a small, gift-wrapped box out of
          his pocket and hands it to Liz.

                    FEAR
          I'd like you to have this.

                    LIZ
          Oh, Harry. For me?

                    FEAR
          Yeah. It's a present.

Liz unwraps the box and takes out a ring.

                    LIZ
          Oh, Harry. What a beautiful ring.

                    FEAR
          Yeah, it used to be my
          grandmother's. By now she's probably
          realized it's gone.

                    LIZ
          Harry, I have to tell you...

The PHONE RINGS. Fear reaches for it, his hand passing the cat skeleton, an objet d'art. Fear speaks into phone.

                    FEAR
          Fear here.

          HYGIENE (V.O.)
          (voice distorted) Hello, Harry.

                    FEAR
          Yeah, Dan?

          HYGIENE (V.O.)
          (voice distorted)
          Harry, sorry to bother you, but we have an
          assignment.

                    FEAR
          I'm sorry, Dan, there seems to be a bad
          connection.

INT. CHEZ MALAISE HOTEL - NIGHT

Hygiene removes his hands from over his mouth and speaks into the phone.

                    HYGIENE
          Sorry, Harry. We've got a big job ahead of
          us, protecting Leo
          Rostelli.

                    FEAR (V.O.)
          Key witness in the Zalluza case,
          right?

>   HYGIENE
>   Yeah. The trial's only a week away and
>   it's up to us to see Rostelli makes it to
>   court alive. You aren't with a girl, are
>   you?

>   FEAR
>   No. Just Liz.

INT. FEAR'S APARTMENT - NIGHT

Fear gives Liz a wink.

>   FEAR
>   What's the address? Six twenty-eight,
>   eight twenty sixth Street. Suite Sixteen.
>   Yeah, I know. Don't tell anybody, not
>   even someone I trust.

Liz perks up.

>   FEAR
>   Okay, I have to stop by the station first.
>   Be there in about an hour.

Fear hangs up phone. He rises from sofa.

>   FEAR
>   Sorry, honey. Duty calls.

>   LIZ
>   Something to do with your job?

Fear puts on his trenchcoat and hat. Liz rises from sofa.

>   FEAR
>   Yeah, I gotta go protect a key witness in
>   the Zalluza case. You know how it is.
>   Goodnight.

Fear gives her a polite kiss and turns to leave.

                              FEAR
          Oh, before you go, could you turn out the
          lights, water the plants, wash the dishes,
          do the laundry, take out the garbage, scrub
          the toilet, and reupholster the couch? I
          appreciate it, dollface.

EXT. CHEZ MALAISE HOTEL - NIGHT

Seedy aging motel. Only some of the neon lights out front work. They
spell "H E L L."

INT. HOTEL CORRIDOR - NIGHT Fear heads to room sixteen.

He greets a UNIFORMED PATROLMAN sitting outside the door on
guard duty, shows his badge and enters.

INT. HOTEL ROOM - NIGHT

The room is filled with POLICEMEN.

Fear walks over to the phone near the door, picks up receiver and dials.
After a moment--

                         FEAR (into phone)
          Oh, and wax the floor. Thanks, dollface.

Fear hangs up. Hygiene walks over to greet Fear.

                              FEAR
          How's Rostelli?

                            HYGIENE
          Fine and dandy.

Fear takes off his coat and throws it on a chair.

LEO ROSTELLI (50), short and scrawny, emerges from the bathroom
in a gaudy but expensive bathrobe.

                            ROSTELLI
          Well, well. If it isn't Fireman First Class
          Harry Fear.

Fear grabs Rostelli by the collar.

> FEAR
> Don't ever call me that! We were
> transferred!

> ROSTELLI
> Get your hand off me.

> FEAR
> You miserable piece of slime!

> ROSTELLI
> You two-bit flatfoot!

> FEAR
> Roman dog!

> ROSTELLI
> Thracian pig!

Hygiene breaks it up and Fear lets go.

> HYGIENE
> We're here to protect the witness, Harry,
> not rough him up.

> FEAR
> Why can't we do both?

> ROSTELLI
> Don't think I've forgotten you, Detective.
> Because of you I pulled a nickel ride in the
> slammer for counterfeiting Monopoly
> money.

> FEAR
> And I'd do it all over again just for the
> pleasure, Shiv, if that is your nickname.

> HYGIENE
> (to other officers)
> Where is Officer Latrine with that food?

The door opens and Latrine comes in pushing a tray with an elaborate serving set and wine on ice.

Rostelli moves for the tray.

> HYGIENE
> What took you so long?

> LATRINE
> It's not easy to find filet of emu this time
> of the season, Sergeant. Sir.

Rostelli grabs for the wine bottle but Fear blocks him.

> FEAR
> Back off. As much as I hate to, we have to
> check for poison. Officer Trainingschool?

Fear motions to TRAININGSCHOOL, a uniformed patrolman, who comes over to the tray. Fear opens a bottle and pours wine into a glass.

> FEAR
> Here, try this.

Trainingschool takes the glass and gulps it down.

> TRAININGSCHOOL
> A hint of fennel and dried cherry. It has
> very little aftertaste, but lingers on the
> palette. Yet it's imposingly vulgar.

Trainingschool falls stiffly to the floor. Rostelli pushes the tray away in a rage.

> ROSTELLI
> What kind of dump is this, serving red
> wine with emu? I lost my appetite. What
> am I doing here? I gotta be out of my head.
> Every guy who ever tried to testify against
> Joe Zalluza is sleeping with the roly-
> polies. Ritchie the Rat, Willie the Weasel,
> Mickey the Marmoset, Nicky the Guh-
> new.

                    HYGIENE
        You mean new, don't you?

                    ROSTELLI
        It's his nickname. If he wants to
        pronounce the G, let him. I'm sweating
        like a horse. I gotta take a shower.

                    HYGIENE
        Don't worry, Leo. You're safe with us.

As Rostelli turns to walk to the bathroom, a large bull's-eye is on the back of his bathrobe. He goes into the bathroom and turns on the SHOWER.

Fear walks over to a table where four policemen play Yahtzee. Fear takes out a deck of cards and flings it onto the table.

                    FEAR
        No, poker.

Latrine hands Fear a piece of paper.

                    FEAR
        (looks at paper)
        Aluminum siding?

Latrine grabs the piece of paper and turns it over.

                    FEAR
        Oh, thanks. Let's see, the license plate
        check says that her name is Liz Tyler.
        2438 Veterans of Illegally Declared
        Foreign Wars Boulevard. Hmmm. I
        wonder why she wouldn't tell me her
        name or address?

Hygiene joins him.

                    HYGIENE
        What'd you say?

             FEAR
Oh, just talking to myself.

             HYGIENE
That's a bad habit.

             FEAR
I know, that's what I keep telling myself.

A LOUD CRASH comes from the bathroom.

Fear and Hygiene lead everyone to the closed door. Fear opens it and
is repulsed by what he sees. He walks in shaking his head and looks at
the shower.

BATHROOM

Rostelli lies in the tub in a pool of blood.

             FEAR
The old exploding shower massage.
Serves him right for putting it on super-
pulsating.

Hygiene crouches over the body with Fear. Fear removes his hat.

             HYGIENE
Somebody get an ambulance!

             FEAR
No. Better make it a hearse.

Rostelli groans.

             FEAR
A hearse that doesn't mind having people
in it who aren't quite dead yet.

             ROSTELLI
Isn't there something you can do?

>
HYGIENE
Well, I could cover my body with
sardines and let myself be nibbled by
pelicans.

>ROSTELLI
No, something for me.

>FEAR
It's too late for that.

>ROSTELLI
It's my time, huh?

Fading fast, Rostelli grabs Fear's lapels.

>ROSTELLI
Do me a favor, cop. Tell my wife she was
the only one I ever loved, but don't tell her
about those weekends at the downtown
YMCA.

He releases Fear's lapels and dies.

>HYGIENE
He's dead, I fear.

>FEAR
No, I Fear. You, Sergeant Hygiene.

They stand. Fear puts on his hat. Latrine comes to the doorway. As Fear and Hygiene exit, Hygiene obstructs Latrine's view into the room.

>HYGIENE
I'd better warn you, it's pretty ugly.

Fear and Hygiene exit. Latrine, looking in, is horrified.

>LATRINE
Oh, how awful. Chartreuse
wallpaper.

HOTEL ROOM

■ *164*   *The Comedeyphiles*

Fear and Hygiene walk out of bathroom.

> FEAR
> How could they have known? Has
> anybody been up here today?

> HYGIENE
> Nobody but you and those two guys
> dressed as maids who said they had to
> replace the shower head. Could you have
> told anybody?

> FEAR
> No, all I did was take the call and--

Fear realizes something. He heads out.

> HYGIENE
> Hey, what's the matter?

> FEAR
> I have to leave. Can you cover for me?

> HYGIENE
> Sure, I guess. Where are you going?

Fear stops just before the door and puts on his trenchcoat. He turns to face Hygiene.

> FEAR
> I have a date tonight.

Fear exits.

> HYGIENE
> Officer Latrine!

Latrine joins him.

> HYGIENE
> You'd better call the boys
> downtown.

Latrine walks to the phone, but turns back.

                    LATRINE
          You do mean the police, don't you?

Hygiene nods. Latrine walks to phone.

INT./EXT. FEAR'S CAR - NIGHT

Fear drives fast. He stares intently, coldly, at the road before him.

                    FEAR (V.O.)
          I had kind of a feeling about Liz and that
          phone call. A strange feeling. Call it a,
          well, a hunch would be a good word for it.
          Love's a double-edged sword and I was
          grabbing the wrong end. I didn't know
          how she could've gotten word to Zalluza.
          I didn't know why she would want to help
          him at all. One thing I did know was that
          eighty thousand tons of bauxite was
          shipped from Jamaica in 1932, making it
          the world's largest exporter for the third
          year running at the time, but that didn't
          help me now. Now I needed more than
          answers. I needed... more answers. I
          couldn't believe it. It just couldn't possibly
          be true, could it?

Fear's expression sours.

                    FEAR
          Chartreuse wallpaper?!

EXT. LIZ'S HOUSE - NIGHT

Fear knocks on Liz's door. She opens it and is startled.

                    LIZ
          Harry?

                    FEAR
          Surprised to see me?

Liz composes herself quickly.

                        LIZ
Why no, come on in.

INT. LIZ'S HOUSE - NIGHT

Fear puts his hat on a rack near the door.

                        FEAR
Do you know where I've been? No, of
course, you couldn't.

                        LIZ
Of course not, Harry. Is something
wrong?

They walk through the foyer and into the sitting room.

                        FEAR
Only if you call being over-vibrated by a
super-pulsating shower massage wrong.

                        LIZ
Well, there's nothing wrong with it if
you're not dead yet.

                        FEAR
Oh, he's dead baby, believe me. Dead.
Gone. History.

                        LIZ
Don't talk that way, Harry. Use complete
sentences.

                        FEAR
Grammatically correct or not, Rostelli, my
key witness, is dead.

                        LIZ
 Rostelli? Dead? How?

                        FEAR
Dead. Murdered. Shower massage.

Liz turns her back on Fear.

>   LIZ
> What does all this have to do with me?

>   FEAR
> You heard me mention the address when I
> took the call. You were the only one who
> could have known. Add them up and what
> do they spell?

Liz faces him.

>   LIZ
> Stop acting like a cop for a
> minute, Harry.

>   FEAR
> Just to get your address I had to act like a
> cop. I had to. I'd reached a stalemate.

>   LIZ
>   (angered)
> Fine, if that's the way you feel then you
> can deal me out.

>   FEAR
> No, chess.

Sobbing, she turns away. Fear grabs her and turns her around.

>   FEAR
> You were just stringing me along like a
> cheap yo-yo! Up and down, walk the
> dog, forward pass, looping, pop the
> clutch, flying saucer, around the world,
> three leaf clover, split the atom, Buddha's
> revenge, the whole nine yards! I could
> kick myself if my legs were on
> backwards. Why did you do it, Liz?
> Why?

He shakes her violently.

>   LIZ
> Let go of me!

                    FEAR
          Tell me why! Tell me why!

                    EDGEMONT (O.S.)
          As your lawyer, I advise you not to
          answer that.

Shocked, Fear turns to see Edgemont emerge from the shadows.

                    FEAR
                    (to Liz)
          What is he doing here?

                    EDGEMONT
                    (to Liz)
          Don't answer that.

                    FEAR
                    (to Liz)
          Did he put you up to this?

                    EDGEMONT
                    (to Liz)
          Don't answer that.

                    FEAR
          How much money did you have to pay
          her?

                    LIZ
                    (to Edgemont)
          Don't answer that.

                    FEAR
                    (to Liz)
          So this is how it is. As soon as my back is
          turned, you turn your back on me.

                    EDGEMONT
          All the evidence against my client is
          purely circumstantial, and I can assure
          you it will not hold up in court.

                    FEAR
          I can't believe this shyster is your lawyer.

                    LIZ
          That shyster is not just my lawyer, Harry.
          He's my husband.

Fear is stunned.

                    FEAR
          You and... all along... but,
          when... how could... what the... who the...
          why the... huh?

                    LIZ
          Now Harry, what did I tell you about
          using complete sentences?

                    FEAR
          I don't understand. Why do you use your
          maiden name, Tyler?

                    LIZ
          Danger was my maiden name. I changed
          it to Tyler for professional reasons.

                    EDGEMONT
          Yes, Harry. You see, Liz and I have no
          secrets from each other, except for that
          Roller Derby assistant coach I shack up
          with on weekends.

                    FEAR
          Now I get the picture. It's all pretty neat.

Fear looks up to see a framed picture on the wall, Liz bumping into
him at the bar.

                    FEAR
          Liz bumps into me in a bar by "accident".

Fear strolls forward to the next framed picture - that of Fear and Liz on
the couch in front of the roaring fire.

> FEAR
> Then the loyal wife pumps me for
> information, and hubby here gets Zalluza
> out of a tight spot. Perfect. Just one
> problem.

Fear strolls forward to the next framed picture - that of

Zalluza dead in the tub.

> FEAR
> A man is dead.

> EDGEMONT
> A man you were charged with protecting.
> Now, unless you wish to be sued for false
> arrest, I suggest you depart with all
> deliberate speed.

> FEAR
> You couldn't keep me here.
>   (to Liz)
> Maybe you could fool me, but you can't
> fool the man upstairs.
>   (looks upward)
> Can you, Mr. Finkelstein?

Leaning on the upstairs bannister is an ELDERLY GENTLEMAN,
balding and amiable. He smiles casually and shrugs.

> FEAR
> From now on you can look me up in the
> yellow pages under unlisted.

Fear walks to foyer and stands in front of door.

> FEAR
> You two may not belong together, but you
> deserve each other.

Fear exits dramatically.

He reenters with uncharacteristic embarrassment, grabs his hat off the
rack and leaves.

INT./EXT. FEAR'S CAR - NIGHT

Fear drives. He looks emotionally spent.

> FEAR (V.O.)
> I may have forgotten my hat, but there are
> some things a man can't forget. The way a
> beautiful woman brushes her long blonde
> hair over one ear. The way she can look
> you straight in the eye and tell you she
> loves you without batting one of her
> gorgeous lashes. But now there was hell
> to pay and they don't take traveller's
> checks.

A large CRUNCH as the car hits something and jolts upward.

> FEAR (V.O.)
> Who was I kidding? I'd never do anything
> to endanger her. I knew
> it, and they knew it. If that's the way it had
> to be I wouldn't stand in their way,
> although I might trip them from behind.
> (mad at himself)
> What a sap I was. Not just any old
> everyday sap, but the biggest sap there is,
> the kind who gives it all up for a woman
> he can never have. After that a week
> passed and I didn't see them for seven
> days.

INT. PRINTING PLANT - DAY

Footage of newspaper printing plant. A newspaper spins into view. A
screaming headline reads:

ZALLUZA TRIAL TODAY: Prosecution's Case Suffers from Loss of
Key Witness

INT. COURTHOUSE - DAY

On the courtroom door is a sign which reads: NO SMOKING, NO
CAMERAS, NO SIGN READING

INT. COURTROOM - DAY

The bleary-eyed BAILIFF takes a nip from a flask. Clears his throat.

> BAILIFF
> Hear ye, hear ye. All rise.

Everyone in the courtroom rises.

> BAILIFF
> Criminal court is now in session. The case
> of the people versus Joe
> Zalluza. The honorable, uh...

He draws a blank. Picks up the judge's name plate and looks at it.

> BAILIFF
> Walter Cabot presiding.

JUDGE CABOT enters and sits at the bench. Everyone sits.

> JUDGE CABOT
> Due to the death of the key witness for the
> prosecution, the case of the People versus
> Joseph Marmaduke Zalluza, The Fourth,
> is dismissed.

He pounds his gavel.

An ELDERLY LADY, knitting, is aghast.

> ELDERLY LADY
> I left my soaps for this?

Zalluza grins and shakes hands with Edgemont. Fear gives a vindictive glare at Liz.

As people rise and leave, the Fear and Liz Doubles file out with the rest of the jury.

REPORTERS approach Zalluza and Edgemont.

> REPORTER #1
> How about a word for the press, Joe?

He leaves.

> ZALLUZA
> (pondering)
> Verisimilitude.

> REPORTER #2
> Tell us, Mr. Edgemont, is it true that you
> don't give interviews?

> EDGEMONT
> Yes, it is true. You see, while I often find
> that the request for one is not
> unreasonable, I don't find
> it necessary or indeed obligatory to start
> running off at the mouth and sharing with
> reporters my inner thoughts and feelings.
> That sort of thing would make me feel
> vulnerable and downright strange. So
> quite the contrary, it has long been my
> habit to clam up entirely when--

Liz claps a hand over his mouth.

> LIZ
> No comment.

Liz and Edgemont exit.

The reporters go to the DISTRICT ATTORNEY's table.

> REPORTER #3
> Any comment, Mr. District Attorney?

> DISTRICT ATTORNEY
> The prosecution's case was irreparably
> damaged by the murder of its key witness,
> a murder made possible by the
> incompetence of one policeman.

> REPORTER #1
> Could you name that policeman?

> DISTRICT ATTORNEY
> That would be unethical. The District
> Attorney's office is not yet ready to
> implicate Detective Harrison Fear, that
> guy over there, for dereliction of duty.

Fear hears the accusation and turns in shock. He walks out of the courtroom and is set upon by reporters.

> REPORTER #1
> Can we get a few words, Detective Fear?

Fear ignores him and tries to make his way through the crowd of reporters.

> REPORTER #2
> I bet you know more than you're telling.

> REPORTER #3
> Yeah, you can stake the farm that the fur's
> gonna fly before the fat lady sings.

> REPORTER #2
> I say it's three to two Zalluza
> knows something.

> REPORTER #1
> I say it's five to one Zalluza
> fixed the case.

> REPORTER #3
> Seven to four Edgemont's involved.

> REPORTER #1
> Eight to five Zalluza's in it
> alone. Take the points.

> REPORTER #2
> Nine to four Edgemont's in it with the
> broad. Match the spread.

Fear looks over to a huge results board where odds are being updated by a bald RESULTS GUY sporting a white rolled up shirt, a black vest, and a pencil behind one ear.

                    FEAR
          Any odds on me?

                    RESULTS GUY
          Even money romantic involvement with
          the broad, twelve to one
          criminal intent.

                    FEAR
          Got it covered.

INT. PRINTING PLANT - DAY

Footage of newspaper printing plant. A newspaper spins into view.
The headline reads: ZALLUZA CASE DISMISSED

INT. SQUAD ROOM - DAY

Fear approaches Hygiene's desk.

                    FEAR
          Any new leads on the Rostelli case?

                    HYGIENE
          Yeah, a make on one of the
          suspects.
               (reading)
          Male Negro, white, dark hair, brown eyes,
          about 6'1", no distinguishing scars, except
          for a small nick on the inside of his thigh
          which I haven't seen but some of the guys
          have told me about.

                    FEAR
          Anything from forensic?

                    HYGIENE
          Fingerprints were inconclusive.

                    FEAR
          Tricorder readings?

                    HYGIENE
          Insufficient data. Obviously some form of
          energy unknown in this quadrant.

                    FEAR
          Those pictures back from the lab?

                    HYGIENE
          Yeah, these should tell us
          something.

Hygiene takes several pictures out of a folder and hands them to Fear.

                    HYGIENE
          We took them with a concealed camera.

The pictures in Fear's hands are completely black.

                    FEAR
          Well, keep your ear to the ground.

                    HYGIENE
          You get dirty lobes that way, but
          alright.

Von Bulow comes over to desk.

                    VON BULOW
          Harry, I need to talk to you. Now.

                    FEAR
          You mean right away?

                    VON BULOW
          I mean now.

                    FEAR
          That's different. In that case, sure,
          Lieutenant.

INT. VON BULOW'S OFFICE - DAY

Von Bulow stands behind his desk and addresses Fear.

VON BULOW
Harry, you used to be a damn good
fireman.

FEAR
That was before our applications were
straightened out, sir.

VON BULOW
And then you were a damn good cop. You
kept your nose clean, did your job, and
went home. Like every good cop you left
your job at the office. But then you started
taking your job home with you. Pretty
soon you were picking it up for lunch.
Late nights with it over cocktails,
morning afters of embarrassed glances
and hurried good-byes, ski weekends in
the mountains.

FEAR
But I--

VON BULOW
And it began to affect your work. You
were no longer just a cop, but a public
avenger with a badge.
And a silly cape.

FEAR
Don't tell me how to do my job! And
leave my silly cape out of this.
    (he calms)
That's just a smokescreen anyway. You
didn't call me in here to deliver a sermon.
Put your cards on the table! Poker.

VON BULOW
Okay, the low down. The D.A.'s on my
back. He's breathing down my neck. He's
poking my eardrums.

FEAR
Who's running this department
anyway?

                    VON BULOW
He won't take no for an answer, Harry. He
won't take yes for an answer either for
some reason.

                    FEAR
So I'm the fall guy, huh?

                    VON BULOW
A witness is dead, Harry, and somebody's
got to take the rap.

                    FEAR
Meaning?

                    VON BULOW
Clean out your desk.

                    FEAR
You got something to say, say it.

                    VON BULOW
Your services are no longer
required.

                    FEAR
Spell it out for me.

                    VON BULOW
I'm letting you go.

                    FEAR
Give it to me in capital letters.

                    VON BULOW
          (as if addressing a small
          child)
You're... fired.

                    FEAR
          (quickly)
You trying to tell me something?

                    VON BULOW
            Harry, hand in your badge.

Fear resignedly takes badge out of his pocket and hands it to

Von Bulow, who glances at it.

                    VON BULOW
            Harry, this is your fireman's badge.

Fear takes out another badge and hands it to him.

                    VON BULOW
            And your silly cape.

Fear pulls out a flashy red, white, and blue superhero costume complete with cape. On the front of the costume are emblazoned the words "PUBLIC AVENGER".

He hands it to Von Bulow.

                    VON BULOW
            Those are the breaks, Harry. Remember
            though, my door is always open.

As Fear exits the office, he moves past the door torn off its hinges as it lies amidst debris and splinters on the floor.

Von Bulow presses an intercom button on his desk and speaks into it.

                    VON BULOW
            Get me maintenance.

INT. SQUAD ROOM - DAY

Fear walks back to desk area where Hygiene sits.

                    HYGIENE
            What's up, Harry?

                    FEAR
            I've been told to clean out my desk.

                    HYGIENE
Meaning?

Fear puts a large empty box on his desk. As he speaks to Hygiene, he
puts in office supplies, his nameplate, a fireman's hat, raincoat, axe,
fire extinguisher, and two Dalmatian puppies.

                    FEAR
My services are no longer required.

                    HYGIENE
Spell it out for me.

                    FEAR
I've... been fired.

                    HYGIENE
You got something to say, say it.

                    FEAR
What does a man's life add up to? I
couldn't afford to go to a fancy college so I
went to school with the U.S. Marine
Corps, and people spit at me. When I got
back from the desert, instead of a hero's
welcome people spit at me. I go to the
post office and people spit at me. I take
my cat into be fixed and people spit at me.
          (quizzically)
My cat spit at me too.

Hygiene spits at Fear.

Fear stops loading the box and lifts it off the desk.

                    FEAR
Thirty years of a man's life and what does
it add up to? A bucket of spit and two
puppies.

Fear exits, watched by Hygiene. Hygiene walks to Von Bulow's office.

INT. VON BULOW'S OFFICE - DAY

Von Bulow is working. Hygiene confronts him.

>   HYGIENE
> How can you do that to Harry? When it
> comes to being a cop you can't say enough
> about Harry Fear.

>   VON BULOW
> Enough about Harry Fear.

>   HYGIENE
> I guess you can say it. Look, there isn't a
> cop on the force I'd rather be partners
> with. Except for maybe Ballinger, or
> Adams, or MacDowell. At least he
> vacuums his car.

>   VON BULOW
> Listen, I'm just following orders.

>   HYGIENE
> Even if it means innocent people get hurt?

>   VON BULOW
> You can't make an omelet without
> breaking a few eggs.

>   HYGIENE
> What are we, cops or short-order cooks?

>   VON BULOW
> I'm just doing my job.

>   HYGIENE
> If that's the way it works, maybe Harry
> was right.

Hygiene pulls out his badge and holds it up.

>   HYGIENE
> What does this badge mean?

>   VON BULOW
> That you're a policeman of some sort?

                         HYGIENE
            If that's the way you feel then you can
            keep this badge.

He slams the badge on the desk.

                         VON BULOW
            That's Kazinsky's badge.

                         HYGIENE
            I know. I can't afford to quit.

INT. PRINTING PLANT - DAY

Footage of printing plant as a newspaper spins into view. The
screaming headline reads:

"EX-MARINE DETECTIVE LEAVES POLICE FORCE UNDER
CLOUD OF SUSPICION

Harrison Fear May Become Freelance Investigative Consultant Father
Was Closet Alcoholic"

THUNDER.

INT. LIZ'S HOUSE - NIGHT

THUNDER. Lightning illuminates Fear's face. Rain POUNDS
against the roof.

                         FEAR
            Yeah, I remember.

                         LIZ
            The days I spent with you were the
            happiest days we ever spent
            together.

                         FEAR
            Yeah, it all fits perfectly, except for one
            thing.

                         LIZ
            What's that?

                 FEAR
   Marty.

Liz moves her lips but no sound emerges.

                 FEAR
   No, that's an important plot point, they
   have to hear it.

                 LIZ
   He doesn't matter, Harry. I never
   loved him.

Liz moves closer to him. Fear doesn't buy it.

                 FEAR
   Sure.

Liz pleads.

                 LIZ
   We can be together, Marty... uh, Harry.
   It's all up to you.

                 FEAR
   Me?

                 LIZ
   Yes, you could-- take care of it.

                 FEAR
   Take care of it? Wasn't one murder
   enough for you?

                 LIZ
   Harry, don't say that!

                 FEAR
   It's true, isn't it?

                 LIZ
   Yes, but I don't like to hear it.
   (suddenly cold)
   Who are you to talk anyway? You're no
   better than I am.

               FEAR
Maybe, but at least it bothers me.

               EDGEMONT (O.S.)
It would bother me too.

THUNDER.

Fear and Liz turn in surprise.

Out of the shadows walks Edgemont, who strolls to the bar and calmly pours himself a drink.

               EDGEMONT
Forgive me for eavesdropping but I
wanted to listen from the shadows
without being observed. Harry, the reason
for her invitation, she always has a reason,
isn't very romantic. You see, the new D.A.
reopened the Zalluza case and my darling
wife worries the past might, as the saying
goes, spatula enema gopher cheese.

Edgemont sips his drink.

               LIZ
You told me you would cut a deal with
Rostelli, instead you gave the address to
Zalluza.

               EDGEMONT
Isn't she wonderful, Harry? Sometimes
when I look into her pale blue eyes and
think about the man she helped to kill I
wonder how many others there have been.

               FEAR
Who are you to talk? You took an oath to
uphold the law, but became the highly
paid mouthpiece of a murderous mobster.

> EDGEMONT
> True, but somehow it seems altogether
> less agreeable in a beautiful woman, don't
> you think?

> FEAR
> You're just splitting hairs.

> EDGEMONT
> Depends on what you mean by splitting
> hairs.

More lightning.

Liz moves close to Fear.

THUNDER.

> LIZ
> Harry, you don't believe him, do you?

> EDGEMONT
> Do you, Harry?

> LIZ
> He tricked me before, Harry. He's trying
> to trick you now. You know what he's
> like.

> EDGEMONT
> Yes dear, but he also knows what you're
> like.

Liz grabs Fear.

> LIZ
> Harry, do something. He could ruin it for
> the both of us.

> EDGEMONT
> You better do it, Harry.

Fear doesn't respond.

> LIZ
> Harry, don't you see? Our coming
> together was fate. Okay, maybe not fate,
> but destiny. Please, Harry.

> EDGEMONT
> Do it, Harry. And then the only worry
> she'll have is you.

Liz breaks away from Fear and goes to a table. She pulls a gun from her coat pocket.

> LIZ
> If you won't do it, Harry, then I will. It's
> the only way. We'll never be safe as long
> as he is alive. He'll turn me in just to save
> his own neck.

Liz points the gun at Edgemont.

> LIZ
> Put your hands up.

Edgemont places his glass down on the nearby coffee table and raises his hands. Then he bends down, picks up his glass, puts a coaster under it, and raises his hands again.

> EDGEMONT
> If that's the way you feel, then there's just
> one thing I have to ask.

> LIZ
> Yes?

> EDGEMONT
> Do you have any bullets?

> LIZ
> What do you mean?

> EDGEMONT
> Those little things you put inside the gun.

A blinding lightning bolt flashes, followed by a DEAFENING THUNDERCLAP. The power goes out and the house is plunged into darkness.

                    EDGEMONT
          Don't be afraid of the dark, my dear. It's
          what you see in the light that'll scare you.

A GUNSHOT from Liz firing in Edgemont's direction. Lightning illuminates the room.

THUNDER.

                    HYGIENE
          My better half's been asking about you.
          So has my wife. She wants you to come
          over.
                    EDGEMONT
               (childishly)
          Missed me! Missed me! Now you gotta
          kiss me!

From off screen a custard pie comes into frame and hits Edgemont in the face. Darkness.

GUNFIRE. Lightning.

The carnival shooting gallery is set up in the room.

Liz fires furiously at a target. The Barker is heavily bandaged and still woozy. A pizza crust falls down on his head and he falls stiffly out of frame.

Darkness.

GUNFIRE and CRIES for help from the Barker. Lightning.

Fear, Liz and Edgemont are gathered together attentively listening to a large 30's style radio.

More GUNFIRE and CRIES for help. Darkness.

CRIES FOR HELP STOP. THUNDER.

Lightning.

A group of Gulf war-era soldiers are in the middle of the room. One speaks into a walkie-talkie unit.

> SOLDIER
> Choppers, pronto! Medic, pronto! Dr.
> Felix Pronto, ear, nose and throat man!

Darkness. Lightning. Strange Guy opens the door.

> STRANGE GUY
> Harry, you've changed!

He closes the door and darkness returns. GUNSHOTS.

Light comes on from a giant torch held by a bearded Viking. Edgemont comes into frame and blows out the torch.

Liz fires GUNSHOT at him. Darkness. Lightning.

Four uniformed policemen are seated at a table playing Yahtzee.

Fear takes out a deck of cards from his pocket and throws it on the table.

> FEAR
> No, poker.

Darkness. GUNSHOT. Lightning.

Fear, Liz, and Edgemont are all dressed in full Western garb, shooting at each other.

Young Fear and Young Edgemont are also present. Liz fires furiously from a Gatling gun. Lightning. Darkness.

The Doubles are now present.

Everyone else is wearing cowboy garb, but Fear and his Double wear fedoras and trenchcoats. They exchange fedoras.

The pace quickens. Darkness. Lightning.

Fear is dressed in the Public Avenger costume. Edgemont is dressed as a Viking.

Everyone else in Gulf war-era fatigues. Lightning. Darkness.

The soldiers are now dressed as Vikings while the kids wear

Public Avenger costumes.

Liz and her Double are Hawaiian hula dancers. Skid Row Wino is on the couch. He takes a swig. Edgemont in fedora and trenchcoat.

Fear and his Double are cowboys. They exchange Stetsons. Darkness. Lightning.

Fear and Edgemont are dressed as fops from the court of Louis

XVI, replete with powdered wigs and pantaloons.

The kids are cowboys.

The soldiers are hula dancers.

Edgemont wears the Public Avenger costume.

Liz and her Double in Viking getup. They exchange helmets. Darkness. Lightning.

Liz and her Double in the Public Avenger costume. The soldiers wear powdered wigs and pantaloons. Fear is a Viking.

The kids are hula dancers.

Fear's Double is dressed as Patton in full regalia. Edgemont is naked, except for covering his crotch with a fedora.

Everyone frantically exchanges hats. Hats fly in every possible direction.

Edgemont looks around nervously, denies all offers to trade with him.

Fear and his Double grab for Edgemont's hat. Darkness. Lightning.

All are dressed in ancient Roman tunics.

Fear and Edgemont, in horse-drawn chariots, face off in a pose reminiscent of "BEN-HUR".

EXT. ROMAN BATTLEFIELD - DAY

An ancient Roman legion battles a Carthaginian horde.

EXT. CIVIL WAR BATTLEFIELD - DAY

Union and Confederate forces fight.

EXT. CARTOONLAND - DAY

Ignatz Mouse flings a brick at Krazy Kat.

EXT. ANTHILL - DAY

Two ant armies wage war.

BOMBARDMENT OF IMAGES:

Charlton Heston as Moses parts the Red Sea; A leopard lunges at a chimpanzee; Brezhnev waves from the Kremlin; "American Gothic"; Jane Fonda as Barbarella;

A subliminal "DRINK COLA" ad; Bob Hope entertains troops; A subliminal "DRINK COLA" ad again; Charles Lindbergh poses before his plane; two German shepherds; F. Scott Fitzgerald dances with his wife and daughter; The Maharishi Mahesh Yogi; The 1921 Miss America pageant; Adam West and Burt Ward as Batman and Robin; Howdy Doody; Oscar Wilde; Alice and the Mad Hatter; the Sphinx; The subliminal "DRINK COLA" ad; the Michaelangelo snowman; Life Magazine photo of audience watching 3-D movie; Rudolph Valentino; Elvis Presley shaking hands with Richard Nixon; "DRINK COLA"; Veronica Lake and Alan Ladd; The Beatles crossing Abbey Road; Pat Sajak.

INT. LIZ'S HOUSE - NIGHT

Lights are back on. Only Liz, Fear and Edgemont are present in their normal clothes.

Liz points the gun at Edgemont, but Fear stops her before she fires.

> FEAR
> Don't shoot him.
> (pointing up)
> The lights are on.

Darkness. A solitary GUNSHOT. The lights come back on.

Smoke pours from Liz's gun.

Edgemont lays dying. Fear bends down to him.

> EDGEMONT (weakly)
> I guess that bullet had my name on it. In really tiny letters.

> FEAR
> Is there something I can get you?

> EDGEMONT
> How about a new spleen?

Fear looks around room and then at Liz. He glances back down to Edgemont.

> FEAR
> So let me get this straight. All this was... for money?

                    EDGEMONT
        It was a nasty fight between the writers,
        the director and the producers, and the
        producers won. Said the audience
        wouldn't be sophisticated enough to
        understand anything else. Elitist a-holes.
        Personally, I liked this whole angle about
        me being abducted and traumatized as a
        child, but alas guess we can't have
        everything.

Edgemont dies.

Liz puts the gun back in the coat on table and joins Fear. He stands.

                    LIZ
        I got a reason, too. One that doesn't
        require any sophistication
        whatsoever.

                    FEAR
        Yeah? What's that?

Liz reaches for his crotch. Fear's eyes bulge.

                    LIZ
        Don't you see, Harry? We're free. Now
        we can be together.

She lets go.

                    FEAR
        Can we? What kind of future would it
        be? The police would hunt us down, and
        if they didn't, the past would.

                    LIZ
        Harry, you're only saying that because
        you mean it.

                    FEAR
        Yeah, I mean it. I mean it just as much as I
        did when I told you I love you.

                    LIZ
But we can be together and forget about
the past.

                    FEAR
I can't forget. I just can't
forget. You can't escape the past. The past
is never dead. It lives with you and goes
wherever you go. The past would be part
of our future.
          (looking at body)
Even if you never thought about Marty--
          (looking at Liz)
--I would.

                    LIZ
Marty doesn't matter. It's you that I love.
Doesn't that mean anything?

                    FEAR
To me it does, but who else have you
played this scene with?

                    LIZ
Nobody, Harry, nobody. I swear it. There
were others, others incredibly talented
lovers, I've never denied it. But you,
you're different. You're no Sherman,
you're vastly different from Carl, Leonard
doesn't hold a candle to you, William's
got spark, but he
doesn't have--

                    FEAR
Alright, alright! I don't care. I don't care
if it's one or a million. Marty's dead and
someone's got to pay for it. Ya hear me?

Liz recoils in shock, turns her back on Fear.

                    LIZ
Harry, you don't know what you're talking
about.

She recovers and turns to face him.

            LIZ
If you love me, you'll trust me, Harry.

            FEAR
I trusted a woman once.

            LIZ
Really? Who?

            FEAR
             (taken aback)
You.

            LIZ
Oh, yes, that's right.

            FEAR
Trust you? I love you. But I
can't trust you. As much as I want to I
can't, because there's a world out there, a
world of blood and tears, of smog and
asphalt, of men and women with all the
passions and frailties that make life a
thousand- to-one shot. You can't hide
from the facts, those cold, hard facts,
because they'll catch up with you. And if
you can't face the facts, you can't face
yourself.

            LIZ
Don't tell me about the facts, Harry. I've
faced the facts, the coldest, hardest facts.
Fact one, a girl is born in Stretch Marks,
Montana. Fact two, this girl grows up and
arrives in Big City with nothing but
ambition and a pretty face. Fact three, she
meets a Mr. Martin Edgemont, on the
outside a well-heeled lawyer, on the
inside a well-heeled lawyer. Fact four, she
marries him and develops a taste for the
good life, taking to money the way a
razorback hog takes to corn slop.

            FEAR
Don't confuse me with the facts. Marty's
dead, and someone's gotta take the rap.

                    LIZ
Marty? Marty was nothing. A two-bit
shyster in a three-piece suit.

                    FEAR
He was a man. And you killed him.

                    LIZ
Yes, I killed him. I killed him to protect
myself. Sometimes a woman has to fight
for what's hers, even if it belongs to
someone else.

                    FEAR
We've all had it tough, babe. But life is a
man's own, to give or take as he chooses.
It's not up to
you to make that decision.

Liz embraces Fear and Fear braces himself. She runs her fingers
through his hair. So does he.

                    LIZ
Remember how it was for us, Harry? It
was beautiful. At that moment I realized
we should be together, forever. We were
just two lonely people with two lonely
hearts until...

                    FEAR
Until?

                    LIZ
Until we met each other. And that's the
only truth I care about, our truth. You and
me. Us. Don't you see, Harry? It can be
the way
it was before in a way it's never been.

Fear pulls away from her.

                    FEAR
Maybe you love me, and maybe I love
you, but what's that got to do with us?

             LIZ
After what we meant to each other? How
can you say that?

            FEAR
Because I'm not the same man who loved
you ten years ago. I'm his evil twin
brother, Garrison Fear.

            LIZ
How can you say that?

            FEAR
I'm taking voice lessons.

            LIZ
But Harry, don't you have any feelings?

            FEAR
Sure, I'm human like most people. But
I'm turning you in. Get your coat. It's a
mite cold out.

Silently, Liz walks over to get her coat. She walks back and faces
Fear.

            LIZ
Just one last kiss, Harry? For what might
have been.

Fear simply looks at her. She inches closer and kisses him. As they
kiss, Liz pulls the gun out from her coat pocket and points it in Fear's
back.

A SHOT RINGS OUT.

Liz falls, revealing Fear holding a gun, smoke pouring from the barrel.

Liz crumples to the ground, dying. Fear turns to go.

            LIZ (weakly)
Why?

> FEAR
> Why not?

Liz dies.

Fear exits.

INT. INTERROGATION ROOM - NIGHT Fear sits at a table, unshaken.

> FEAR
> ... and I drove through the rain until I got
> here. That's about it.

The table is surrounded by several firemen in full garb. A dalmatian sits nearby.

Fear rises to leave.

> FEAR
> See you later, boys.

They return his farewell as he leaves.

INT. FIREHOUSE - NIGHT

Fear walks down the hall of the fire station and is mildly surprised to be met by Hygiene.

> FEAR
> Hiya, Serge. What are you doing here?

> HYGIENE
> My house burned down. Just came back
> from the Edgemont place. It wasn't pretty.

> FEAR
> Murder seldom is.

> HYGIENE
> You know, Harry...

> FEAR
> Yeah?

Fear stares at him.

>   HYGIENE
> Fact is, she's got this cousin she's trying to
> marry off. Don't get me wrong, Harry,
> she's a nice girl. Pretty. Good cook too.
> Makes wonderful sheep dip. You can
> come over, eat, maybe play some
> Yahtzee.

>   FEAR
> Been a while since I've played Yahtzee.

>   HYGIENE
> In that case you're on my wife's team.
> Sunday. Six-thirty.

Fear nods. Hygiene exits.

Fear walks through the corridor.

>   FEAR (V.O.)
> Stardate. One Nine Eight Nine Point Four
> Six. I was alive and two people were
> dead. But I couldn't cry too much because
> I knew it might just as easily have been
> me.

Fear walks toward the exit.

>   FEAR
> Death is a funny thing. Sometimes I
> wonder what I would do if I knew I only
> had twenty-four hours to live. I guess I'd
> probably spend them like they were my
> last day on Earth. Yeah, there's a thin line
> between life and death. But the thinnest
> line of all is the one between love and
> hate. Somehow I had managed to erase
> that line. Lucky for me it wasn't written in
> magic marker.

EXT. FIREHOUSE - NIGHT

Fear walks out of the fire station. The rain has stopped. He pulls his collar up against the cold and walks to the street.

> FEAR (V.O.)
> You can't be afraid of the dark, because
> the night is always dark, and no matter
> how dark the night, eventually the bright
> light of morning will shine on the new
> day.

Fear walks onto street and alongside a small firetruck. He gets in and drives off into the Big City night. Alone.

FADE OUT.

Chapter 12

FATE IS MY DESTINY

(This treatment is a summary of the as-yet-unwritten sequel to THE NIGHT IS ALWAYS DARK.)

Night. Shadows fall on the dark city streets. We see a lone figure lurking - unkept, unshaven. It is Harrison Fear. How did he get into such a mess?

Flashback. The private eye business is bad, so Fear has taken on a new partner, Rex King - a garrulous, hail-fellow-well-met type, in contrast to the taciturn Harry.

Fear and King are hired by an invalid millionaire, Colonel Brickwood (who uses a cane even though he is in a wheelchair), to tail ne'er-do-well gambler Dallas Houston, whom the Colonel suspects is having an affair with the Colonel's nubile young daughter, Belinda. The detectives also meet the Colonel's voluptuous young wife, Cleo, who says Dallas is a no-good swine.

Fear and King tail Dallas Houston to the racetrack and various gambling joints (lots of interesting visuals in these scenes) as well as checking in with Sgt. Hygiene of the Big City Police Department. They also talk to Belinda, who swears her love for Dallas and "would rather see him dead than with another woman." Dallas calls Fear and sets up a meeting at the racetrack. Fear goes and finds Dallas murdered -- and Fear is seen by witnesses over the body. He fights his way out and is a hunted man.

The dragnet is out in Big City for Harrison Fear. He calls Rex King to touch base . Cleo is also in the office and tells Fear to meet her at a safe spot. Fear trusts her and goes to the meeting place, only to find it crawling with cops. Fear realizes Cleo set him up and calls King warning him. King sets up a meeting with Fear at a deserted amusement park outside town.

Fear shows up and sees King. Relieved, Fear then hears a familiar voice: Cleo. Cleo was having an affair with Dallas, who threatened blackmail. Cleo got Rex to help her, she was warned of Fear's meeting by King and killed Dallas. Now Fear must die. Suddenly, the power in the park is turned on. Fear is able to run. Rex and Cleo chase him, but they end up dead. The power was turned on by Belinda (who followed Cleo). Belinda runs to Harry and hugs him, saying all this was good because it introduced her to the man she wants to marry: Sgt. Hygiene.

Fear walks into the Big City night. Alone. Again.

Chapter 13

❦

CARTOONS APLENTY

The appendix section of my book THE JOKE'S ON YOU: HOW TO WRITE COMEDY contains a list of cartoon situations. The list was compiled after doing a lengthy study of the wonderful cartoons of The New Yorker magazine. Going through a collection of gags from our files (with the help of a friend) I compiled a list of gags. Gags are brief description of the situation, people, and what the caption will be. From there I found an excellent artist online, Jonathan Brown, who did all the artwork contained in this chapter. Hope you enjoy this section.

"Something tells me I ought to bid on this one."

"But on the other hand, I'm my own boss."

"I think they're onto us."

"Rough day at the office, Dear?"

"I'm happy to report our downsizing program has been a complete success."

"The murderer is somewhere in this room."

YOU ARE NOW LOST

"Who ordered the pepperoni?"

"Ours is not to reason why, ladies and gentlemen.
Ours is but to introduce a scenario of plausible deniability."

"I think these Civil War reenactments have gone too far."

"I regret that I have but nine lives to give for my country."

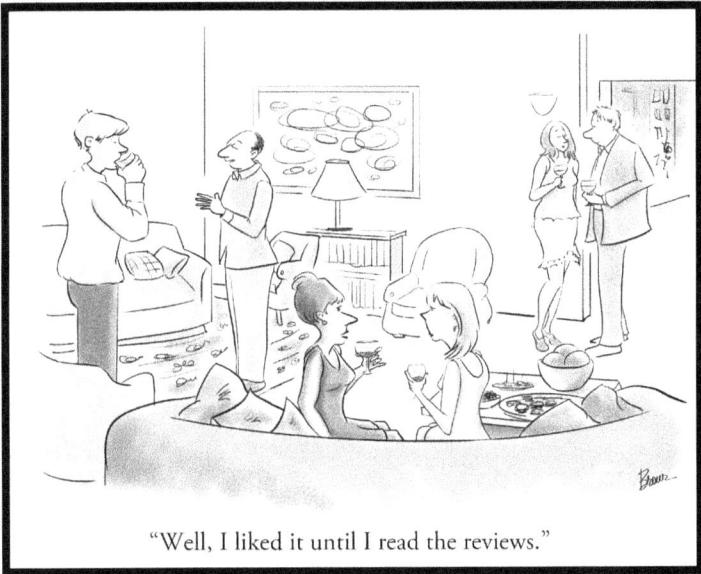

"Well, I liked it until I read the reviews."

"MIT fan."

BOOKS ON VIDEO

"Garcon, a bottle of your cheapest champagne!"

SHAKESPEARE IN THE PARK

"Throw that lunatic out, he thinks he's a psychiatrist!"

"Of course, I'll need you to sign a document for tax purposes."

"Popcorn. Peanuts. Get your red hot peanuts!"

REMBRANDT GOES BAROQUE

"Okay, I'll give you a financial statement: I have no money."

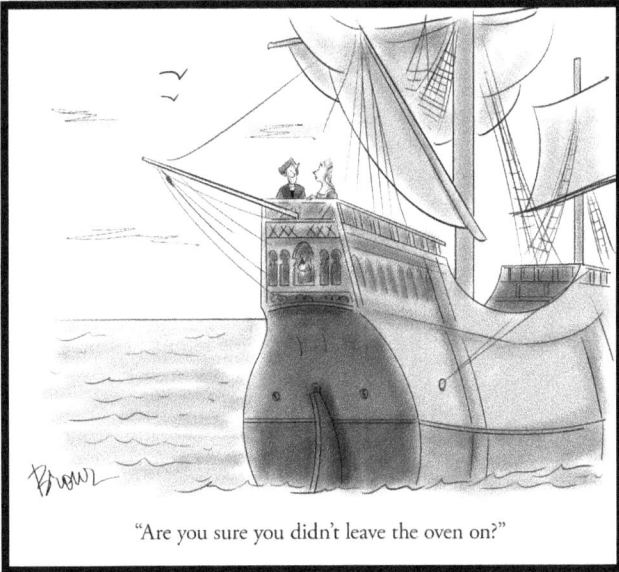

"Are you sure you didn't leave the oven on?"

"If life were a painting, my Walter would be a still life."

"They don't seem to be biting today."

"He refuses to talk."

"And if you'll look to your right, you'll see the captain and copilot parachuting to safety."

"You can't bluff me. I know you're out of ammunition."

"Just take the damn stroke penalty, Hugh."

"I must say, you're the most persistent
insurance salesman I've ever met."

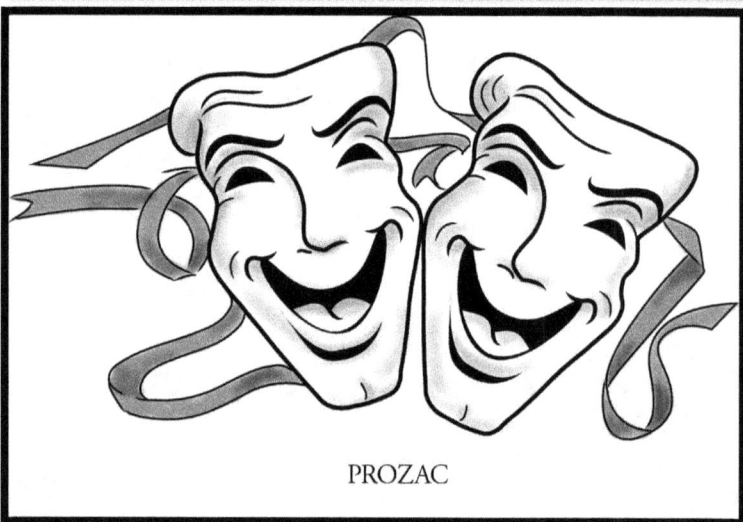

PROZAC

"Your novel has an incomprehensible plot, witless dialogue, and reads like a four year-old wrote it. Have you considered turning it into a screenplay?"

"You're getting too much fiber."

"His grammar is appalling."

"Plundering is down 26%."

"No, no, no! This land is your land, ***this*** land is my land."

"Impressive as it is, your collection of string
is not acceptable as collateral."

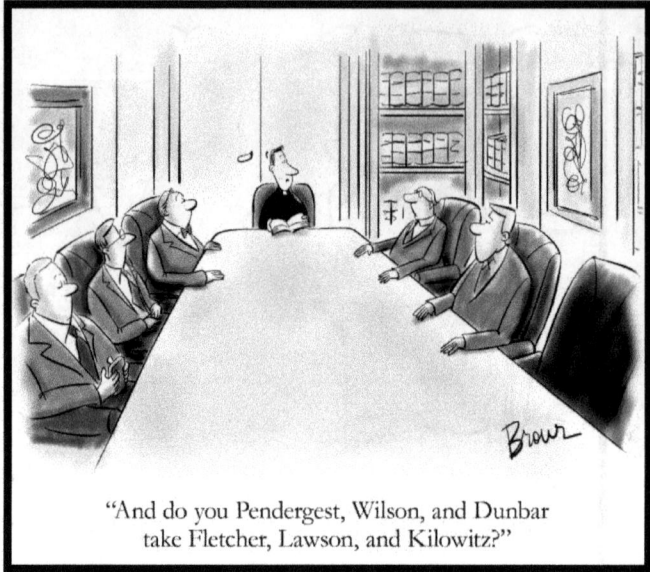

"And do you Pendergest, Wilson, and Dunbar
take Fletcher, Lawson, and Kilowitz?"

"You little piggies can go to the market for roast beef,
but this little piggy is going home."

"Do you take requests?"

"Having scratched your surface, Jenkins,
we're not really interested in what's beneath it."

"I detect an undercurrent of hostility."

"I'd like an ounce of prevention, please."

"Gerald has yet to optimize his potential."

"If you say, 'Water, water everywhere' one more time..."

For a comprehensive study of comedy turn to Amazon's top selling comedy writing book:

The Joke Is On You: How to Write Comedy.

Available at Amazon.com in Kindle or deluxe paperback edition.

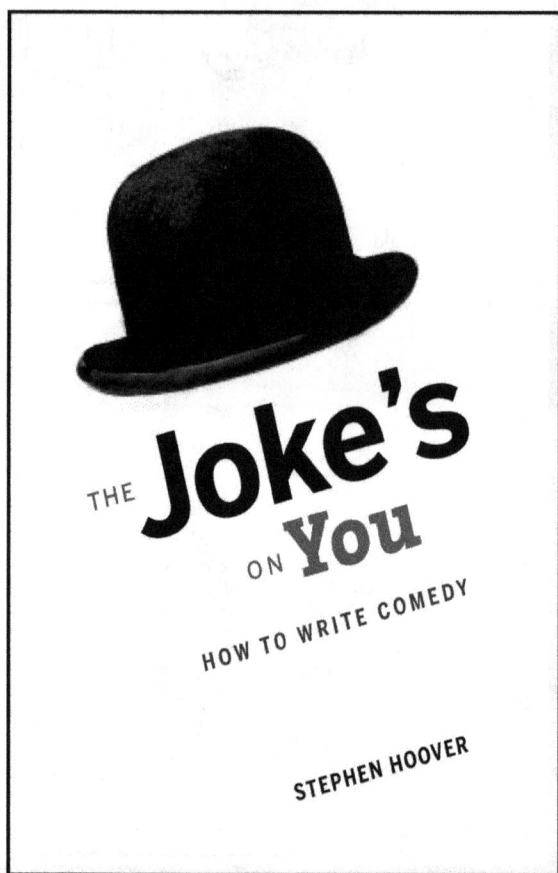

www.ingramcontent.com/pod-product-compliance
Lightning Source LLC
Chambersburg PA
CBHW070953040426
42443CB00007B/484

9 780989 746540